SPEAKING *Of Success*

INSIGHT PUBLISHING
SEVIERVILLE, TENNESSEE

SPEAKING *Of Success*

Disclaimer: This book is a compilation of ideas from numerous experts who have each contributed a chapter. As such, the views expressed in each chapter are of those who were interviewed and not necessarily of the interviewer or Insight Publishing.

Published by Insight Publishing Company
P.O. Box 4189
Sevierville, Tennessee 37864

10 9 8 7 6 5 4 3 2

Printed in the United States of America

ISBN: 978-1-60013-121-2

Table of Contents

A Message from the Publisher

When we decided to do a series of books on success, we searched long and hard to find just the right combination of authors who were not only a success in business but were successful in their personal life as well.

The authors we found had personal stories to tell that revealed their inner values—values that contributed to the achievements they have made and the positive influence they have on others. These authors are people whom others revere as persons of integrity. They are winners.

Everyone wants to be a winner. I have never met anyone who wants to be a loser. And I'm sure you haven't either. That's why we found some of the best motivational/inspirational speakers and authors in the country to contribute to this series. Some of these men and women are household names. Others are rising stars. All of them have achieved the kind of success all of us want—the kind that sparks enthusiasm in others and leaves an indelible, positive impression.

The road to success is one of hard work and persistence. *Speaking of Success* can help you unlock your potential and inspire you to realize the many possibilities awaiting you as you learn how to remove any mental blocks you might have to the success you deserve.

If you're already well on your way down the success highway, the stories and experiences of these authors will encourage you, inform you, and I guarantee that you will learn something.

It is with great pride that we Insight Publishing present this series, *Speaking of Success.* We think you will discover that you will find something new each time you read through these books.

The chapters in this series are real page-turners, so get ready to be inspired. Get ready to be delighted. Get ready to learn. And remember, *you* are the author of your own success journey. Others can shine a light on the path but you must do the walking.

Interviews conducted by:
David E. Wright
President, International Speakers Network

Chapter 1

ELLEN PURCELL

THE INTERVIEW

David Wright (Wright)

Today we're talking with Ellen Purcell. Ellen is a Master Teacher and Trainer of the internationally renowned PAIRS program, which offers communication and relationship classes for couples around the world. Specifically, Ellen leads the PAIRS 120-hour Relationship Mastery Program with her husband, Chuck, in their training center near Washington, D.C. Additionally, as a PAIRS Professional Trainer, Ellen certifies professionals around the country to conduct PAIRS classes. Ellen has lectured at George Mason University, James Madison University, and George Washington University. She has presented workshops, television, and radio shows, and there have been several articles in newspapers and magazines featuring her work with PAIRS, including a front page article in the *Washington Post.*

How would you define a successful couple's relationship, Ellen?

Ellen Purcell (Purcell)

It is a relationship where both people are willing to be attentive to each other's feelings and needs, and to prioritize their time every day to include nurturing the relationship. Once they have made the commitment that they will make time for each other—as they used to do when they first met—then they need to have the understanding about how healthy relationships work. They then need to have the skills of how specifically to handle the stresses, differences, compromises, and frustrations that are natural in all close relationships. And last, but certainly not least, that successful relationship would include loving each other.

If it is a successful relationship, each person would feel loved, cared about, needed, compassionate, and would be willing to speak up (in a skilled way!) about their own needs, and would want to really listen to know about their partner's needs (with the expectation that they will be different), and have the understanding that the approaches to solving any given problem will be different and will usually need to involve compromise.

Wright

What do you think are the biggest obstacles to couples being successful in their relationships?

Purcell

Underneath the lack of skills and understanding I already mentioned, one primary obstacle to success in relationships comes to mind: Fear. It may not look anything like fear in our behavior, but that is the root of it. It's the fear of not being loved, not being lovable, fear of being alone and lonely, fear of not having the basic human need met for connection with someone who really cares. This fear shows up in so many ways that are destructive to our close relationships, that often we don't recognize it.

If we don't think we are really lovable (this can fly in the face of tremendous "business success," wealth, and accolades), we may sabotage those who try to be close: the "best defense is a good offense"—"If I push you away, you won't leave me once you learn that I'm not lovable" or "If I let myself get close in a relationship, my fears may tell me to try to control you to insist that you do things my way, so hopefully you will stay and take care of me." Fear like this often shows up as anger or as guilt-inducing manipulation with tears or as distancing—"If you leave, I won't miss you that much." There are so many variations, but under it all is the fear of not being loved or lovable.

Wright

How do you know what couples need to do to have a successful relationship?

Purcell

I was wonderfully blessed about fifteen years ago to study with the creator of PAIRS, Dr. Lori Gordon, and to learn how to present the classes and apply its principles in my life every day. In teaching these classes, I saw the proof in front of me over and over again with our participants. PAIRS is an acronym for the Practical Application of Intimate Relationship Skills. I love that it has so many concepts to teach participants about how this relationship puzzle actually works, as well as so many specific practical skills to apply to just about every possible situation life may toss at us.

So, to restate that, I know what couples need because I was taught by Dr. Gordon, and a cadre of geniuses who worked with her who contributed to the underpinning of PAIRS theory and skills—including Dr. Virginia Satir, whose pioneering work in this field is woven throughout these programs.

But I also know what works because I see it work in my own life, and for those who apply what this program teaches.

Wright

What is PAIRS and how is it different from counseling or therapy?

Purcell

PAIRS is a relationship education program that focuses on health, not on problems. It is a non-blaming, skills based approach to learn the habits and skills for having successful relationships with all those we are close to. So, in addition to our partners, that would include children, siblings, parents, friends, and co-workers. It is useful for couples to use a solution-focused process such as PAIRS, which prioritizes a "win-win" for each person in the relationship.

We recommend in this approach that there is less time spent on trying to understand what has gone wrong in the past, and much more time learning and practicing specifically what will work for the couple now and in the future.

For individuals who are faced with clinical issues, such as substance abuse, addictive behaviors, clinical depression, or violence, it is advisable that they seek appropriate professional assistance. They need to have these behaviors under control with a professional counselor before a relationship education program like PAIRS can typically be helpful. While classes like PAIRS may be incredibly therapeutic, we consider them educational, not therapy.

The problem has been that often unskilled couples who do not have clinical issues see a therapist when their marriage is in trouble. Then the couple can think, "Wait a minute, I don't need therapy, I just need some skills of how to be in this relationship." Without knowing about programs like PAIRS they leave the therapy feeling that they have "tried everything" and give up on their marriage when what they really needed was marriage education.

This is a sad waste and it is why my husband and I really want couples to know that there is another option.

Wright

What are some of the key steps that couples can take to make their relationship a success?

Purcell

I'm glad you asked. I have come up with ten key ways to have successful relationships:

1. *Learn to listen effectively.* People think they are listening just because they are not talking—but usually our heads are filled with other thoughts about how to respond, stories we have to tell, or other distractions about our lives. Learning how to truly listen is a skill.
2. *Express personal thoughts and feelings clearly.* Often we are filled with ideas that we want to share, but we hold back—sometimes assuming people we care about will just "know" what we want (and even not appreciating when something is done if we had to tell them about it) or guessing that the other person won't want to hear what we want to say. Sharing clearly, without an "attitude," is so important.
3. *Learn, accept, and enjoy the differences between you and your partner.* With all the talk about diversity and tolerance, you would think this is obvious. But what is really true is that in our close relationships, we often expect the other person to think the same way we do, and when they don't, we sometimes try to persuade them to change. If we can say instead, "I'm puzzled . . . I see it differently . . . will

you tell me your ideas about this?" as a first reaction when there are differences, we might learn new things, see different points of view, or sometimes even agree to disagree.

4. *Accept that anger is a natural human emotion—and find positive, constructive skills to handle it.* Hoping we won't argue and get angry with those we love is a very unrealistic expectation. We are all products of different upbringings and beliefs, and we usually have very different approaches to just about everything. Learning the skill of letting out our anger in non-blaming, non-destructive ways *before* we try to come to an agreement about things, is essential to staying close.
5. *Make it a priority to spend undistracted, private time with people you care about.* Even if it is just fifteen to thirty minutes a day—that means no television on, no reading at the same time—just a few minutes to share your thoughts and feelings about the day. This is a critical ingredient to feeling we are in close, caring relationships.
6. *Give a minimum of one genuine appreciation for the other person each day.* It is especially important to *say* words of appreciation (not just think them)—we all need to be recognized for the good things we do. If we only hear criticisms or requests to do things, we do not feel very good. The appreciation needs to be specific and sincere.
7. *Avoid mind reading.* If you think someone is upset, sad, or angry with you—check it out. Say something like, "I noticed you haven't been sitting with me at lunch for the past couple of days . . . are you upset with me about something?" Usually, we assume we know what others are thinking—and then we take action based on that. But we are rarely accurate in our mind reading, and it can cause the relationship a lot of trouble.
8. *Recognize how you react when you are upset.* Often, it is our *style* of reacting to others when we are upset, rather than the issue itself, that causes more of a problem. Try to think if there is a more positive, caring, empathetic way to respond when someone angers you. For instance, if a sales clerk seems to be rude and abrupt with you, instead of making some smart remark or being angry back, you might say with empathy, "It sure is a long day you put in here. I imagine you are ready to go home and get off your

feet!" Often a smile comes out, and the attitude goes away. We have a choice of how we interact with others—especially those we are close to. It is always better to try to have good will and assume the person is doing the best he or she can.

9. *Try Journaling.* It can be on your computer, or in a special notebook—just a private place to write down your thoughts. Recent studies have shown that our physical health is much better when we write down things that upset us—both what happened and our feelings about it. Getting it out and down on paper can give us a different perspective on what bothered us, as well as just feeling some relief to get it out and not hold it in.
10. *Give and ask for lots of hugs.* We all need warm, caring connection with the people we care about. Hugging is not about sex. It is about everyone's need to feel liked and loved—that we are a pleasure to be around just as we are.

Wright

Have you found most relationship challenges able to be overcome? When does divorce seem like the right answer?

Purcell

There are a number of ways to look at this. One is that, as I said before, if there is substance abuse, violence, addictions, or illegal behaviors taking place in the relationship, resolving those becomes the first priority—even if it means separation for safety's sake while healing hopefully can occur.

For most couples we see, however—even the ones who insist they just can't stay in that relationship any longer—often the issues are about misunderstandings, styles of communication, hidden expectations or assumptions they have brought to the relationship or lack of skills in dealing with anger or pain. Those situations and patterns of connection—the bad habits they have been using for most of their lives—can, with commitment, be overcome. New ways of communicating—even when angry—can be learned and used. Couples can fall back in love once the defensive walls are lowered and reconnection is made in a healthy way.

Another thing to consider is that in a recent research study of 5,232 married adults conducted by a team of leading family scholars headed by University of Chicago Sociologist Linda Waite, they found no evidence that unhappily married adults who divorced were typically any happier than unhappily married people who stayed married.

Even more dramatically, the researchers also found that two-thirds of unhappily married spouses who stayed married reported that their marriages were happy five years later. In addition, couples in the most unhappy marriages reported the most dramatic turnarounds: among those who rated their marriages as very unhappy, almost eight out of ten who avoided divorce were happily married five years later.

So, the expectation that divorce will bring happiness is, for most people, a myth. While the stresses of the marriage (that they have not learned to handle skillfully) may be gone, new stresses of being alone, divorced, a single parent, having new financial burdens, etc. take their place. So, rather than divorce, we say put your energies into having your current relationship become successful.

Wright

Have the basics for success in relationships for couples remained the same or changed over the past few generations?

Purcell

They certainly have changed. In earlier generations, there was often much less emphasis on romantic love and personal gratification. Expectations were not as high about "being happy" ahead of other factors. Just a few generations ago, a person's survival, or the survival of the children, usually depended on the family unit staying together and working together. Now, however, because of economic and social changes, men and women can take care of just about all their needs themselves. They can hire housekeepers, single women and men can adopt, and each can earn enough to live on his or her own.

But the one thing we can't do on our own is get our needs for connection, lovability, and intimacy fully met. For that we need another person. So, all the importance we used to place on the other factors of survival, we now place on happiness in relationships. No wonder it seems impossible to find that "perfect person" who will meet all our needs for intimacy—physical closeness, emotional openness, and honesty. Many have decided it just "can't" happen and are staying alone or turning to their pets to give and receive warmth and connection. We are back to that primary obstacle to success for couples that I mentioned before—fear.

With most people thinking their only options are to take their chances falling in love and maybe being miserable in a relationship, or separating and the pain that involves, it is no wonder that so many are opting for avoiding pain. However, there is now that third option—getting relationship education to become emotionally literate, so you can increase the odds of success tremendously in your favor.

Wright

There are hundreds of books and tapes available to teach couples how to be happy. How do they stack up compared to the successes available through learning in a class?

Purcell

I love to read and learn. There truly are many wonderful books, tapes, and programs out there. Each has something special and unique to offer to help people become "consciously competent" in relationships.

In addition, it's true that what many couples really need is the time and focused energy to let what they are learning become a new habit for them. When we talk to couples about taking our PAIRS Relationship Mastery Program, one thing we ask is what they have already done to improve their relationship. Often we hear of one or the other being very enthused about a book with exercises in it to practice—but they tell us that having the discipline to keep doing these things gets lost in the overwhelming demands of life, family, and work schedules.

With our class, participants make a commitment to come and work on learning and practicing new ways to communicate over several months. It is said that a new habit has to be practiced dozens of times before it becomes integrated into our natural response. So whether it is a book, tape, or some other process that teaches the skills needed, the second part is practicing these new skills—habits—over and over until we don't have to think about them. We have found an enjoyable, interesting class over several months to be the easiest and most effective way to accomplish this.

Wright

How can such a personal subject as closeness and intimacy between two people be taught in a classroom setting?

Purcell

That is certainly one of the biggest concerns potential class participants have. They don't want to be embarrassed in front of others, they don't know really what will happen in the class, and they don't have any guarantee that things will be better afterward—back to that big obstacle of Fear!

The way we get around that is twofold. First of all, the class is structured in a way where we understand that initially people will not want to share much with fellow classmates. Concepts are taught to the whole class. Exercises are light and fun and typically involve the couples only sharing with each other. Then gradually, as participants start to open up a little, they learn that basically everyone in the room (including us as teachers) are human, are imperfect, are doing the best we can, and are at various times all struggling with many of the same issues. When that reality is understood, then connection, empathy, and trust naturally build; then some even deeper, more lasting learning can take place. In a lot of ways it can create a "team spirit" in the class where everyone is encouraging and supporting each other to learn, grow, and heal.

Couples who take this approach learn what it takes to have a happy relationship. They practice the skills to use when they are having challenging times, and can feel empathy for themselves as being "not so different" from other couples they have grown to like and respect in the class who are also struggling to have wonderful, intimate, fun relationships. This humanizing process takes away some of the aloneness, takes some of the pressure off, and provides increased energy to work on the relationship together as a couple, rather than one against the other.

We have a saying that "when one person wins, the relationship loses." When couples focus on the "us" and stop focusing on the fear that their own needs won't be met, they can really get to the kind of successful relationship they crave.

Wright

Will you tell me about your experiences in teaching couples how to be close and happy? What has this meant for you personally?

Purcell

Serving as coach to let couples find the loving person inside, having them start to feel more lovable through the processes we teach and understandings they receive in the class, watching an individual take off his or her mask and take down walls of protection is a real thrill. For my husband and me, it is spiritual in a deep meaning of the word. When couples really experience unconditional love and each partner can commit to giving that love to one another and to family, nothing much else in this world really matters.

We have seen couples "fall back in love." The ripple effect on their lives, their family, friends, and the world are not to be underestimated.

Wright

Aren't couples likely to be successful if they can just find the right person—their soul mate—in the first place? Maybe singles should take this class before getting into a relationship?

Purcell

Yes, that question of "finding our soul mate" is an interesting one. I read an article recently that said more damage to relationships has been done in the name of that "one soul mate" concept than can be imagined. This is because it can result in unrealistic expectations about what a successful relationship looks like. We think we can just show up, not give to or nurture the relationship, and it will thrive.

What we need to know is not how to find the perfect partner but, as it has been said, how to *be* the perfect partner—or at least, a wonderful partner. No one is perfect. It's the love we bring and share in a relationship that will open the door for romance, fun, and true happiness.

And yes, absolutely, we love having singles in our classes. Some of our most vocal, enthusiastic supporters of PAIRS are the singles who took the class to learn about themselves and how to be in a close relationship. They also learned what they really need from a partner, how to avoid making their partner pay for pain from their own past, and how to speak more directly about what they liked and wanted. Singles in the class don't waste any energy on trying to point out to a partner that what we are teaching applies to the other person (not themselves) and if their partner "would just fix that problem, everything would be fine." They are there for themselves to learn what they need to know.

Once they have finished the program, they are very clear about what a successful, healthy relationship looks like, and can focus on making that happen—especially the part they bring to the relationship's success, rather than just hoping they will meet that "perfect person" who will make everything right.

Wright

In case our readers wanted to learn more about PAIRS classes, what is the best way for them to do it?

Purcell

Well, the easiest way to find out about how to achieve relationship success through our programs would be to visit the PAIRS Foundation's Web site: www.PAIRS.com. There is a directory of the nationwide PAIRS leader network and a calendar of upcoming classes with full contact information. To reach us in the Washington, D.C., area people can visit www.PAIRSVirginia.com.

Whether you are in your twenties or your seventies, single, separated, or married, you owe it to everyone you know (and to yourself!) to find out how to have a consciously competent, emotionally literate, happy relationship with all those you are close to—the ripple effects could change the world!

About the Author

In 1997, the national office of the PAIRS Foundation awarded Ellen Purcell certification as a PAIRS Master Teacher. From a field of thousands of trained PAIRS professionals, there are currently fewer than twenty-five leaders who have attained this level of certification. Ellen leads the PAIRS Relationship Mastery Program with her husband, Chuck, in their training center near Washington, D.C.

Additionally, as a PAIRS Professional Trainer, Ellen certifies practitioners around the country to conduct PAIRS classes. Ellen has lectured at George Mason University, James Madison University, and George Washington University. She has presented workshops, television and radio shows, and several articles in newspapers and magazines have been written about her work with PAIRS, including a front page article in the *Washington Post*.

Ellen Purcell
PAIRS Virginia
1900 Campus Commons Drive, #100
Reston, VA 20191
Phone: 703.476.5644
E-mail: ePAIRS@aol.com
www.PAIRSVirginia.com

Chapter 2

STEVEN FULMER

THE INTERVIEW

David Wright (Wright)

Today we're talking with Steven Fulmer, a Human Strategist and creator of LifeQuest Mapping™, a dynamic program that helps companies and organizations capitalize on their human asset. It provides practical tools, solutions, and methods for powerful decision-making, taking control of one's life, and removing the barriers between where they are and where they want to be. He started his first successful business in photography at the age of sixteen. By thirty-five Steven was vice president in a $10 million software company he helped grow from $300,000 a year. He regularly appears on the ABC/KATU morning show, *AM Northwest.* He brings his more than twenty years of business experience to his professional speaking, workshops, and personal/executive life coaching as he helps individuals and organizations strategize paths to success by gaining new perspectives so they can take action.

Steven, welcome to *Speaking of Success!*

Steven Fulmer (Fulmer)

Thank you, I'm happy to be here.

Wright

I've put this question to a lot of people and I get almost as many answers as people I've asked: what is your definition of success?

Fulmer

In a single word I define success as "happiness." There are contextual definitions of success. For instance, business success might be running a profitable business. If you are successful in athletics, it might be winning a national championship. If you're successful in love, it might be receiving a "yes" to a marriage proposal or finding your soul-mate. But underlying all those contextual definitions lies something deeper, something at a more core level that allows all of those things to occur. I call it happiness.

It's interesting when I throw that word out to people because sometimes happiness is perceived as naïve or shallow, lacking a certain depth or recognition of the challenges that life can present. Happiness is also interpreted as one-sided, meaning only the joyful side of life without consideration for sorrow. One person called it a "cheap sell." But I have found that happiness does not exclude sorrow or the full range of emotions that life inspires. In fact, happiness cannot live without them. It is neither easy, nor naïve and it is by no means a "cheap" sell. I am shocked by how many people sincerely fight happiness, feeling they aren't worthy or that the pursuit of their personal happiness is somehow selfish.

When I do workshops and ask how many people are happy—truly happy—it's amazing how few hands go up or how many respond with, "Well, I'm not *un*happy," or "Are you kidding? I've got three kids and a mortgage, who's got time for happiness?"

Maybe it's because of my Catholic upbringing but I, like a lot of people in the world, have thought throughout my whole life that I was born to do something specific—that I was put on this earth for a specific reason—and the first step is figuring out that purpose. That lifelong search for my purpose was quite the burden. As a result, I saw success as the achievement of this ultimate purpose. I kept searching and thinking, "I'm twenty, twenty-five, thirty, thirty-five, years old—what am I supposed to be doing with my life? How can I be successful if I don't know what I am supposed to be successful *at?"*

Many people have responded to me, "Yeah, I know exactly what you mean!"

It was shortly after the birth of my first daughter, following the national tragedy of 9/11, that it became clear to me—I'm looking at the question all backward—instead of "what" am I supposed to do with my life, I began asking *how* am I supposed to be in my life? The answer is brilliantly simple: be happy! The Dali Lama wrote a book on it, Bobby McFerrin sang a great song about it. I believe that happiness is what got buried in our national psyche when the towers fell that mournful September day in 2001. Happiness is what I dreamed for my daughter as I held her in my arms six months later fretting and dreaming over the responsibility my wife and I had just created.

When I said to a friend, who was lamenting that same struggle for purpose, that her purpose was to be happy she laughed. So I said, "Think about it, when you're happy the world is an amazing place, right? When you are happy doesn't the sun seem brighter and the clouds seem less oppressive? When you're happy, you wake up with more energy. When you're happy, little things don't bother you, you are more forgiving and less judgmental. When you're happy you have more brainpower and you can come up with solutions that you didn't see before. When you're happy, you have excess energy to do beautiful things like art and laughing, or volunteering and philanthropic endeavors. When you're happy you can believe that all things are possible—and it is contagious!"

When you're unhappy, however, everything's much more difficult. You wake up saying, "I *have* to go to work," instead of, "I *get* to go to work." You think, "If I had extra money I would feed the hungry or volunteer at a children's shelter," but you don't. Little things bother you disproportionately. For instance, someone cuts you off in traffic and it ruins your whole day. You use phrases like "you make me so mad!" even though you understand intellectually that no one can "make" you mad. When you're unhappy you have no excess energy, there's no extra drive left to really make a difference in the world or find a true "purpose." When you are unhappy, so much of life is about getting by, keeping your head above water, or making ends meet.

When you are happy things simply make more sense.

I sometimes get responses such as, "But that's not success. I've seen unhappy people do successful things." I almost agree—I've seen unhappy people accomplish things, but I would challenge if they are successful or not, and I admit, this has a lot to do with the standards by which one judges happiness and success. However, if these "unhappy" people can achieve great things when they are unhappy, how much more could they accomplish if they were truly happy? Or more importantly, how would they impact the world more significantly if they were happy? Just because an unhappy person achieves something, does that mean he or she is successful? Even a broken clock tells time correctly twice a day! Accomplishing something—is that success or is that achievement? These are two very different things.

Consider it this way: if your success is achieving some great purpose in life, what are the odds that you will only have one purpose? Statistics indicate that students graduating from college today will have between seven and eleven different careers between graduation and retirement. This shows that human beings are creatures of diversity. You may actually have several great purposes in life and succeed at a great many things but what if you can't find them because you are suffering in unhappy misery, lamenting what is missing, or negatively judging the experiences you must pass through first?

There's a great bumper sticker that says, "All who wander are not lost." Likewise, not knowing what you are meant to "do" does not mean you are lost, confused, or on the wrong path. Achievement is an evolutionary process. Just as you can't drive from Oregon to New York without passing through many different states, perhaps even with a few wrong turns along the way, your greatest achievements will come as a result of experimentation, mistakes, and many miles over the roads of life. The question is: how are you experiencing the living and the journey? Are the mistakes, miles, and experiences along the way viewed as failures or part of the greater success?

Success, by my definition of happiness, is not a state of naïve bliss, but the state of being completely conscious and deliberate in your living. It is the state of being so fully awake in your life that you truly experience your life. In this state of success you feel all levels of emotion from great joy to great sorrow with the operative word being "feel."

The doing will happen in your life whether you like it or not. You will get jobs, people will cut you off, you will unexpectedly find a $20 bill in your winter coat, and you may marry and have kids whether you are conscious or not. After all, many people move from the cradle to the grave on auto-pilot believing that life happens to them. They are victims or at the least, observers. But with this awakening, this awareness of your life, you gain a power—you realize that all things are possible and you seek the best of what life has to offer and offer life the best you have to give.

I've been asked if I am advocating an acceptance mentality where the outcome doesn't matter and one simply needs to have a positive attitude about one's life. I'm neither suggesting that you should settle for an undesirable result nor am I suggesting that you rationalize an outcome in order to be or pretend to be "happy." What I am saying is that the outcome is neither the definition of success nor it's opposite—that which we often call failure. You can actually not get what you want and not be satisfied with the result and yet still feel successful or happy because each decision you made along the way was made consciously and in alignment with your values and intentions. You might wish the result was different, but that doesn't diminish the "success" of living life by your terms: consciously, deliberately, and fully awake.

Success in the end has less to do with *what* you achieve and more to do with *how* you respond to the journey and the outcome. That's what my program LifeQuest Mapping™ is all about—how to respond to life, the universe, and everything.

Wright

I am intrigued by "LifeQuest Mapping™" what is that exactly?

Fulmer

LifeQuest Mapping™ is a methodology for figuring out how to make empowering choices, take exciting chances, and build a rewarding future. Go back for a moment to this idea that so many people believe there is an ultimate purpose for their life. I meet a lot of people who come to my workshops on a "quest" to figure out what their purpose is as if it's a destination. Therefore, when they hear "map" they see in their minds eye a treasure map—a string of riddles and clues that lead to a giant "X" marking the spot filled with the treasures of life. The destination is their goal and what they seek is the path, convinced that if they had the map they would find this hidden treasure chest and it will be filled with all the wealth they seek, whether that wealth is financial, spiritual, emotional, relational, or any combination thereof.

When you pick up a real map, it doesn't tell you where to go because a real map isn't about a single destination. A map is about endless possibilities built around three pragmatic principles: figuring out where you are, determining where you want to go, and choosing how you want to get there. So LifeQuest Mapping™, and thus success, is ultimately about addressing those three principles. But real life is messy and seldom goes according to plan; that's why a map can be so valuable.

Imagine if your goal was to drive to Kansas and you thought you were you were in Kentucky; you would start heading west. However, if you were actually in Oregon, heading west will land you in a large body of water that you didn't expect. In reality, many people don't really know where they are or where they are going, or worse yet, they believe they are one place (e.g., Kentucky), when in fact they are somewhere else (e.g., Oregon). As a result, the path they choose causes them to get lost or miss their destination completely because they aren't starting from an accurate starting point. The point being, if you do not know where you are, you can not get where you are going. The same is true in life.

Here's an example: Take a woman who has dreamed about marriage her whole life and finally, at the age of thirty she gets married. The problem is she expected holy matrimonial bliss, a committed friend, lover, and dependable companion. What she didn't plan on was the part of her she was leaving behind—the freedom of being single, the ability to eat dinner over the kitchen sink without a plate, or leave her pantyhose hanging over the curtain rod. The things people struggle with most in their marriage become the things they left behind or the things that didn't live up to their life-long expectations within the marriage. They didn't start the marriage from a clear understanding of what marriage is—they started from where they thought marriage should be, or how they wanted it to be without consideration of the realities of having someone else in the equation.

No matter what journey you take in life you are leaving something behind. Some of those things are good to leave behind, like the lonely Saturday nights or the constant nagging of family and friends wondering when you will be getting married. Other things will be missed, like the freedom that comes with being single or the fairytale visions of how marriage should be. If a person does not take stock in the full range of truth in where he or she is, it is tantamount to starting a journey from an inaccurate starting point. To get anywhere in life, you must first know where you are.

The challenge in life, however, is that even if you start from an accurate location, somewhere along the way you will encounter an obstacle—the road is closed, or the bridge is out—thus preventing you from reaching your destination the way you intended. In real life it might be not getting a promotion or having an accident in your new car. Unfortunately, many people view those obstacles as evidence that they're not allowed to have their goal. Some even use it as proof that they can't achieve what they want until something external from themselves changes in their life. Success is the ability to take charge—pull out "the map" and find a way around the obstacle or discover the lesson in the experience—and feel positive about your actions instead of succumbing to the obstacle's impediment.

The idea of LifeQuest Mapping™ (LQM) is literally that—building a map for your life that is very specific to who you are, understanding what kind of obstacles you face, and the routes around them. Then when you wake up one day with a vision or a purpose, you have a tool to get there from anywhere in your life.

Wright

Am I correct in my understanding that you are not talking about traditional goal-setting?

Fulmer

Absolutely, LQM differs dramatically from goal-setting because goal-setting is mostly about achieving something. For instance, someone may decide to set a goal to be a millionaire by forty, or break an athletic record—that's about achieving something. What happens if you don't achieve it? Does that mean you are unsuccessful? Let's say you sell cars and your goal is to sell twenty cars this month. What happens if you only sell fifteen? Are you a failure? Are you not successful? Compared to the guy who only sold five cars you are three times as successful—if success is based on achievement. However, what if you sold twenty-five? Mathematically you missed the goal by the same amount—five over, five under, either way you missed the goal by five—but you feel better about the five over, don't you? Of course, everyone likes to exceed expectations. But that's the point, expectations and achievements are not success, they are expectations and achievements. Five over and five under are both 25 percent off your mark; the only real difference is how you "feel" about it. Sure, exceeding your goal by 25 percent makes your boss happy, but anyone in sales knows where that leads you—to a bigger goal! What if the greed leads you to a goal you can't achieve; are you then a failure or unsuccessful?

Many people, especially Americans, are all about the drive and the achievement. As a result, they put on blinders, put their head down and go forward into their goal full force, missing so much along the road of life and failing to enjoy the outcome because once it's achieved they are on to the next goal. Whereas success is more about the experience in route to the goal, seeing the big picture and viewing the detours and obstacles of life as part of the success rather than an impediment.

Consider the car sales example again. What is a better outcome for a dealership, selling fifteen cars to customers who love the experience, who view the dealership as honest and trustworthy, and then go out and tell all their friends what a great experience they had? Or selling twenty-five cars to people who felt disrespected or poorly treated and walk away feeling like they were just another sale, complaining about "typical car salespeople," and never recommending the dealership. How one feels about an experience or achieving a goal has a great deal more value then the result. Consider the movie *Cars*. The character Chick Hicks ended up winning the Piston Cup, but Lightening McQueen, who sacrificed the victory to help The King finish his last race, was far more successful.

In 1991 I moved from Long Island, New York, to Portland, Oregon. I chose to drive across country because all my life I dreamed of driving across country. Along the way, near Gothenburg, Nebraska, there was a sign for the last remaining Pony Express Station museum. I was traveling with my mom and we looked at each other and said, "Well, it's the last one, we've got to check it out." It took about forty-five minutes of driving from the time we saw the sign until we got there. By the time we arrived it was dark and the museum was closed. We sat there in the dark in the middle of the neighborhood that had grown up around the museum and said, "That was a waste of time."

While we are talking in the cab of the truck we heard a tap, tap, tap on the driver's side window. Outside was a little old lady motioning for us to roll down the window. I lowered the window and she instantly began speaking at the speed of light: "Hello, I am curator of the museum and this is my dog Brandi and I saw you pull into the neighborhood and I knew you would be disappointed that the museum was closed . . ." She talked on and on and on and she proceeded to give us the entire history of the Pony Express, concluding with an invitation back to her house.

We ended up spending more than an hour with this incredible woman, and had one of the most remarkable experiences of our lives. We were enthralled with learning about her family and the history of the area. In a short span of time she reminded my mom and me about life, family, people, and the trust and magic of strangers. We got back in the truck to drive on and my mom and I looked at each other wondering what had just happened. "We just met an angel," I said. When we arrived in Oregon I wrote a letter to the *Gothenburg Times,* the local newspaper, and told them about their "Angel of Gothenburg."

More than a year later I got a letter from the curator's daughter. She wrote a beautiful letter sharing that her mom had recently passed away and she wanted us to know something. Her father had died a few years earlier and her mom had never been quite the same. After my mom and I left Gothenburg, her daughter said her mom came back to life in a new way. There was seldom a day that passed when she didn't talk about *her* angels from Oregon or refer back to the letter I had written to the paper. "In some ways you gave us back our mom," her daughter told me, "and your letter to the paper meant the world to her." In this letter from her daughter I came to learn how much I had meant to this woman in the months following our random visit. I learned how much she spoke of us and the meaningful impact of my letter to the paper.

We would never have met our angel had we not taken the detour to look for the last remaining Pony Express Station. She had said it was a beautiful, heart-felt letter I had written to the paper and it clearly touched her. All along I thought *she* had been a gift to *me*. I had no idea the impact that I had on her!

The moral of the story is, if you're just about goals, if your head's down and your focus is only on the destination, it's difficult to take the detours and extemporaneous excursions in life. It's hard to see the other possibilities; it's hard to trust your instincts when it's not about the goal. Goal-setting is good and necessary, but it's not success. Success is about having the tools to find focus, value, and meaning no matter what happens or what detours life throws at you. You will always be able to get back on track confidently knowing there is always a way to reach your desires regardless of the obstacles, and knowing that sometimes life's best experiences come from the detours or maybe even missing the mark. It's about being happy and experiencing all that life has to offer in route to what you are trying to achieve.

Wright

What do you think is the largest obstacle standing in the way of people's success?

Fulmer

The largest obstacle is a two-sided coin. On one side is the failure to believe and on the other is the power of choice. On the first side is the failure to believe in one's truth, the failure to believe in one's possibilities, the failure to believe in oneself, the failure to believe that one deserves what one desires, the failure to believe that one's view of one's life is vastly superior to the opinion of those around him or her, and the failures in belief roll on.

Through the voice of *Hamlet,* Shakespeare said, "There is no good or bad, but *thinking* makes it so." To the unsuccessful, life is all about good and bad; unfortunately they see mostly the bad because they *think* others control their life, that's why they use statements like "You make me mad!" Or, "How can I soar like an eagle when I am surrounded by a flock of turkeys! My co-workers make me look bad." Unsuccessful people know all these reasons why they are not happy and why they are not "successful." Nearly every one of those reasons has to do with people and circumstances outside of themselves. How many times have you heard someone say, "I would be successful if—" and they have a litany of reasons how and why other people are standing in their way? It's the "you can't get there from here" syndrome.

When I was in Wales I was planning a holiday trip to Ireland. A Welsh friend said to me, "Have a great time, just don't ask an Irishman for directions."

"Why not?" I asked.

"Because," he replied, "they'll just tell you that 'you can't get there from here.' They'll start by saying you've got to go down the lane to the oak tree, make a left, follow the path until you get to the old stone church, and make a right, then you can get where you want to go."

We both laughed; it was funny. Then years later it dawned on me—that's how unsuccessful people live their lives: "I can't get there from here." "Something else has to happen *before* I can get what I want." "I'm not allowed." "I don't come from the right family." "I'm not the right gender." "I'm not the right color." "All these people are holding me down," or, "If these people would just do their job then I could—" or, "If I could just win the lottery." "If I just had the money." There are all these conditions that have to be met, separate from themselves, for them to be successful. They believe there are insurmountable obstacles between where they are and where they want to be.

Here's the bottom line to this belief point: if you don't believe you are worthy of happiness, if you don't believe you are worthy of success, if you don't believe you deserve what you desire, you cannot become what you dream about. I have said for years that the recipe for success is to "Dream, Believe, Become." You can only become what you believe you are and what you believe you are worthy of. If you believe you are incapable or someone else has to do something or something else has to happen—you can't get there from here—then you're right, you will not become successful in whatever incantation that looks like to you. But if you do believe, then all things are possible.

The biggest obstacle standing in the way of people's success is what they believe to be true. The flip side of that coin is choice.

There is an old joke that says, "Everyone needs to believe in something, so I believe I'll have another beer." So be careful in what you believe. It is very easy to use this power of belief against yourself. Choose powerful things in which to believe because where the rubber of beliefs meets the road of choice is at the intersection called decision. If you believe that the next decision you make in your life will be tantamount to the single most important decision you will make in your life, then it will carry the weight of the world, and the pressure and stress that goes into that decision will cloud your vision of possibilities.

Any decision in your life—what to declare as your major in college, where to go to college, whom to marry, what job to pursue, or whether to turn left or right at the stop sign—is merely a decision. Any decision is simply that: the next decision. No matter how important it may seem, there will always be the result of that decision and with the result comes the gift of the next decision.

This leads me to the biggest piece advice I give people: judge not the decisions of yesterday with the knowledge of today. Learn from the past—absolutely. Judge yourself for the result—absolutely not. Today you know something you did not know yesterday—the result of your decision. If you had that insight yesterday you may have made a different decision. That doesn't make yesterday's decision wrong; it simply makes it a decision. Remember what Shakespeare wrote, "There is no good or bad, but thinking makes it so." Now, with your newfound knowledge, forget the judgment of good and bad and make a new choice.

Until you are dead you always have a fighting chance to change. Once you realize that today is the net result of every decision you have ever made in your life, you realize that tomorrow will include the result of every decision you make today. Life is like the stock market—past performance is no indication of future gains. While real life may not have any "do-overs" it has plenty of tomorrows; believe that you control those tomorrows through your beliefs and choices about today and you can succeed at anything. So if you wake up and find yourself in a different place than you intended to be, learn from the past, examine your beliefs, and choose how you want to live your life in a way that honors your values and your truths.

Wright

I can see how one's beliefs can really hold one back, but I imagine these obstacles can bump into some pretty powerful fears. So how does one face the fears that these beliefs conjure up?

Fulmer

Fear is another big obstacle. We are also largely misled about fear; its role in our life and what happens to it. I make my living, and have for nearly twenty years, doing public speaking in some form or another. The funny part is that as a youth I faced the same debilitating fear that most of the world faces: the fear of public speaking.

When I approached graduation from high school my dad asked what I was planning to do. I said I didn't know. I thought I was going to pursue my interest in photography because that's where I was "successful" at the time.

"Are you going to college?" he asked.

I told him I would go to community college because I didn't know what else to do; I was going to experiment.

"Great," he said, "take a public speaking class."

When I was done laughing I said he had to be out of his mind, there's no way I was going to take a public speaking class. "There's nothing I'm going to do that's going to require me to stand in front of people and speak," I said.

"You don't know that," he replied.

"Oh yes I do," I countered, "Because I know I'm never going to make a choice that involves public speaking."

After an hour and a half discussion I finally agreed to take the class. "But if I fail," I warned him, "I don't want to hear a word out of you!"

He laughed and said, "No problem."

On the first day of class, the first assignment was to speak from a topic in the class textbook. I came home furious because I disagreed with every premise that the book put forth about public speaking.

"Well," Dad said, "did the teacher say you had to agree with the book?"

After a long pause and a dumfounded expression on my face, I said, "Uh, no . . ."

"Then say what you think."

"I can do that?"

"Of course you can do that."

"What if I get a failing grade for doing that?"

He said, "So what if you fail?"

"Are you saying that's okay?"

"I'm not saying that at all," he replied. "If you disagree with the book and that's what you think, speak from what you believe."

The next day at class five students spoke before me and talked about the topic of listening. They repeated exactly what the book said, which was basically that the audience should pay attention, sit up, not allow themselves to be distracted, and not do other things. I thought it was all insane! This was a class about public speaking, and I thought my job as a speaker was to get the audience's attention, give them incentive to want to listen, and to say something worth putting their distractions down for.

So when I stood up before the class I stated my topic—"Listening"—and everyone groaned and slouched in their seats. I then said, "Yeah, but I disagree with the book and the five people who went before me." Everyone sat up in their seats! Instantly I had them hooked—I had their attention. Suddenly it wasn't about public speaking anymore, it was about public thinking. I was able to express my opinion, and when my dad gave me the gift of removing the fear of failure, which really amounted to the judgment of failure, suddenly the reward of public thinking became greater than the fear of public speaking.

In order to face one's fear one has to change one's perspective. People must be able to see something different about the situation in which they are afraid.

Imagine if you were looking at the Earth from outer space. Your location would determine everything you could see. From one perspective it would look like almost all water. From another perspective it would look like almost all ice. From another perspective it would look like all the Americas from north to south, and from another perspective you would see China and Australia. Perspective is everything! No single perspective is right or wrong—it just "is."

If you are afraid the Earth is icy and cold, find a new perspective. If you want to overcome a fear, find a new perspective! Look at things differently. If you can see things differently, then suddenly reality begins to shift.

When you can find something in a new perspective that allows you to be stronger in a new belief than the fear was in the old belief, you can achieve remarkable things! Look at me, I'm a speaker now. I stand sometimes in front of thousands of people talking about various topics. When I was six years old I knew I wanted to change the world, and I couldn't do that remaining silent. As I grew I learned to hide behind the lens of a camera for fear of public speaking and the inability to believe in the value of my opinions. Fear—it's a powerful emotion, but it's not the absence of fear that allows great things to happen. Courage, they say, is not the absence of fear—it is action in spite of fear.

Fear is not always bad. It can keep you safe and make you smarter, but the difference between positive and negative fear lies not in the fear, but in its role.

I love sailing so I ask the question in this way: There are many "ships" in your life: Relationships, Leadership, Scholarship, Companionship . . . The question is: who is the captain of your ship? If fear is your captain, if fear is calling the shots, and if fear is the motivation behind whom you choose to listen, your ship is likely never going to leave the dock. But if fear is a healthy and trusted crew member that is there to give you an honest report that you will factor together with the reports of other crew members such as adventure, hope, skepticism, excitement, nervousness, and love, then you have power. Fear then becomes a valuable tool. Facing your fears is seldom about eliminating the fears, and is almost always about putting them in perspective.

That's what I did regarding public speaking. I found a new perspective that was stronger than the perspective of fear, which is still there; it's what keeps me sharp and respectful of my audience. I now choose different things in which to believe and as a result I am fulfilling a dream I have had since I was six—to change the world.

Wright

So, is perspective the secret to success?

Fulmer

Perspective is how you find success. Perspective can either empower you or give your power away. If you understand the fact that perspective is how you're seeing your world, then your success is based on your own perspectives of yourself. For example, if you see yourself as limited, if you believe that you can't, or if you're convinced that something else has to change for you to get where you're going, then how can you be successful by any definition of the word?

However, if you can step back and look at life from the point of view of true personal happiness (i.e., a place of control and conscious living), then you can be successful at anything because success isn't dependent on the outcome.

Happiness is a place of being fully aware. It's a consciousness of who you are, meaning what you truly value deep inside and why you value it. When you look over your life at the greatest and the worst moments can you identify what it is about those moments that honor or dishonor a certain truth about you? When you can recognize those truths, you begin to gain perspective and take control.

Who you are has so very much to do with how you feel. Explore the feelings you experience during the powerful moments of your life from winning a championship or graduating with honors to losing a loved one or a battle with drugs and you will find happiness. Sometimes it shows up first through an understanding of what makes you *unhappy*, and if that happens, spin it around and look for the other perspective. Find what is missing in the unhappiness and you find a perspective that can lead to happiness. Every front has a back, every top has a bottom, and every in has an out. Look for them all; there are always alternative perspectives. Then choose the perspective you really like, the one that honors the life you want to live and be known for, and seek the evidence from this point forward that supports that perspective. Success is totally a function of perspective—change your perspective and you change your world.

Wright

So what if you disagree with alternative perspectives? Isn't that where conflict arises?

Fulmer

That is where potential conflict can arise; it all depends on which perspectives you choose. There's an old expression that says, "A mind once expanded cannot return to its original shape or dimension." By looking at all perspectives, or many at least, you are going to come up with alternatives that don't make sense to you, that you don't agree with, or you would never follow, but you will find someone else who does. In doing so, do you realize what you just gained? Insight!

Imagine meeting someone with a different perspective, one you considered but rejected in favor of a different perspective. What a gift! Why? Because you have already recognized that alternative perspective as valid, as one that exists. There is no need to argue about the truth of this alternative perspective, so instead you can explore each other from a place of curiosity, seeking to understand what it is about that perspective others connect with because, just as you have settled on your perspective, they have done so as well. As a result, you can reach a place of acceptance. This is key: *acceptance is not agreement.* You can accept the existence of alternative perspectives without agreeing with them because they no longer reflect on your position. They become independent forces—neither is dependent on the other.

A sailboat's objective is to get to its destination, and the wind's objective is to blow in whatever direction it darn well pleases. It doesn't matter to a sailor what direction the wind is blowing—he does not have to change the wind in order to get where he wants to go. Even if he wants to go in the opposite direction of the wind, there is a way to do it! It's called "tacking." He can go back and forth and back and forth until he arrives at his ultimate destination. That's cooperation. The sailboat takes nothing from the wind, and the wind gives nothing up, yet both achieve their ultimate goal.

You might point out that the wind just blows, but the sailor has to tack—isn't the sailor in some way caving in to the perspective of the wind? That is one perspective. Another perspective is that the wind is not the conscious half in this analogy, it's just blowing. The one who is fully aware, conscious, making deliberate choices about his or her destiny and figuring out how to succeed without causing harm is the sailor. The sailor can reach any destination he or she desires and is no longer being blown by the winds of change or thrown off course because someone else has a different perspective or life threw up an obstacle the sailor didn't expect.

When you come across these alternate perspectives, whether publicly or internally, instead of looking at them as conflicts, obstacles, or proof that "you can't get there from here," ask yourself what perspective will serve you here? What is the path you can take to get to where you want to be?

Wright

So am I hearing that perspective and success has an element of the art of negotiation?

Fulmer

Yes, I would agree there is an element of the art of negotiation. At first, success is about finding your happiness. It doesn't matter what you define happiness to be, it's about being true and honest with yourself, and it's about clarity, self-respect, and conscious and deliberate choices with your eyes wide open.

I once heard that "negotiation is the art of letting someone else get your way," which is funny as a joke, but that's not negotiation because it gives no respect to the other side. Negotiation by its very nature is a "win-win" scenario; anything else is coercion. If you accept this premise about success equaling happiness, then you accept that it is also true for everyone else. If it is also true for everyone else, then negotiation is about having respect for all. It's allowing your success to thrive while letting someone else's success thrive even if it differs from yours, and it's about finding the point of cooperation where everyone is served, just like the wind and the sailboat.

Wright

What is the one thing that you want people to take away from your message about success in this book?

Fulmer

Harry Chapin is one of my all-time favorite musicians. He sang "Cats in the Cradle," and "Taxi"—among many other beautifully profound songs. I heard a radio interview with him where he told a story about his grandfather. All his life Harry's grandfather wanted to be a painter, and though he painted a lot he wished he had been more "successful."

The grandfather told Harry about the difference between what he called "good tired" and "bad tired." "Ironically," he said, "bad tired could be a day when you've won, but you've won other people's battles, you fought other people's wars, you lived other people's dreams, and when you lay your head on the pillow at night you toss and turn, because there was very little 'you' in there."

He said, "Ironically a good tired can be a day when you lost, but you lost fighting your battles and living your dreams and when you lay your head on the pillow at night you 'sleep the sleep of the just' knowing that you lived your life your way, true to who you are."

I wish for people a "good tired"—living their lives their way, following their dreams, believing in their possibilities and power, with the ability to look into their own heart and know at the end of the day, regardless of the outcome, that they lived for themselves, their purpose and their value.

I'm an ordinary guy with an extraordinary vision. I believe compassion and respect are vital ingredients to purpose and action, which grows out of the place of one's knowing and understanding of themselves. The more people acquire the core foundation of success—happiness and the ability to touch deep emotions of all types—the more they are able to accept others for who they are, the more they are able to find hope, dream seemingly impossible dreams, and change the world. Success creates achievement. Find happiness as I have defined it and you will stand in a place of self-confidence and knowing. Alternative perspectives and contrary beliefs will no longer be a reflection of you, but an empowering place to practice insatiable curiosity and seek sincere understanding. Then, like the sailboat and the wind, success becomes a universal reality instead of an individual achievement.

Success is the power to see the vision, create opportunities, empower yourself and others, and set the wheels of change in motion. Success is what comes before and carries on long after a goal is achieved.

Wright

What a great conversation, I really appreciate your taking all this time with us, Steven, to answer all these questions. I have learned a lot.

Fulmer

Thank you, I've really enjoyed this. This was a lot of fun.

Wright

Today we have been talking with Steven Fulmer who has over twenty years of experience as a professional speaker, workshop facilitator, and trainer. Steven helps people gain new perspectives about their lives and to take action.

Steven, thank you so much for being with us today on *Speaking of Success!*

Fulmer
Thank you very much, it was my pleasure!

About the Author

STEVEN FULMER is a Human Strategist and creator of LifeQuest Mapping™, a dynamic program that helps companies and organizations capitalize on their human asset. It provides practical tools, solutions, and methods for powerful decision-making, taking control of one's life, and removing the barriers between where they are and where they want to be. He started his first successful business in photography at the age of sixteen. By thirty-five Steven was vice president in a $10 million software company he helped grow from $300,000 a year. He regularly appears on the ABC/KATU morning show, *AM Northwest.* He brings his more than twenty years of business experience to his professional speaking, workshops, and personal/executive life coaching as he helps individuals and organizations strategize paths to success by gaining new perspectives so they can take action. Steven lives in Portland, Oregon, with his lovely wife Julia and two daughters.

Steven Fulmer
LifeQuest Mapping™
P.O. Box 91284
Portland, OR 97291
Phone: 503.526.2011
E-mail: Steven@StevenFulmer.com
www.StevenFulmer.com

Chapter 3

DR. KEN BLANCHARD

THE INTERVIEW

David E. Wright (Wright)

Few people have created a positive impact on the day-to-day management of people and companies more than Dr. Kenneth Blanchard, who is known around the world simply as Ken, a prominent, gregarious, sought-after author, speaker, and business consultant. Ken is universally characterized by friends, colleagues, and clients as one of the most insightful, powerful, and compassionate men in business today. Ken's impact as a writer is far-reaching. His phenomenal best-selling book, *The One Minute Manager®*, co-authored with Spencer Johnson, has sold more than thirteen million copies worldwide and has been translated into more than twenty-five languages. Ken is Chairman and Chief Spiritual Officer of the Ken Blanchard Companies. The organization's focus is to energize organizations around the world with customized training in bottom line business strategies based on the simple, yet powerful principles inspired by Ken's best-selling books.

Dr. Blanchard, welcome to *Speaking of Success*!

Dr. Ken Blanchard (Blanchard)

Well, it's nice to talk to you, David. It's good to be here.

Wright

I must tell you that preparing for your interview took quite a bit more time than usual. The scope of your life's work and your business, the Ken Blanchard Companies, would make for a dozen fascinating interviews. Before we dive into the specifics of some of your projects and strategies, will you give our readers a brief synopsis of your life—how you came to be the Ken Blanchard we all know and respect?

Blanchard

Well, I'll tell you, David, I think life is what you do when you are planning on doing something else. I think that was John Lennon's line. I never intended to do what I have been doing. In fact, all my professors in college told me that I couldn't write. I wanted to do college work, which I did, and they said, "You had better be an administrator." So I decided I was going to be a Dean of Students. I got provisionally accepted into my master's degree program and then provisionally accepted at Cornell, because I never could take any of those standardized tests.

I took the college boards four times and finally got 502 in English. I don't have a test-taking mind. I ended up in a university in Athens, Ohio, in 1966 as an Administrative Assistant to the Dean of the Business School. When I got there he said, "Ken, I want you to teach a course. I want all my deans to teach." I had never thought about teaching because they said I couldn't write, and teachers had to publish. He put me in the manager's department.

I've taken enough bad courses in my day and I wasn't going to teach one. I really prepared and had a wonderful time with the students. I was chosen as one of the top ten teachers on the campus coming out of the chute!

I just had a marvelous time. A colleague by the name of Paul Hersey was chairman of the management department. He wasn't very friendly to me initially because the Dean had led me into his department, but I heard he was a great teacher. He taught organizational behavior and leadership. So I said, "Can I sit in on your course next semester?"

"Nobody audits my courses," he said. "If you want to take it for credit, you're welcome."

I couldn't believe it. I had a doctoral degree and he wanted me to take his course for credit, so I signed up.

The registrar didn't know what to do with me because I already had a doctorate, but I wrote the papers and took the course, and it was great.

In June 1967, Hersey came into my office and said, "Ken, I've been teaching in this field for ten years. I think I'm better than anybody, but I can't write. I'm a nervous wreck, and I'd love to write a textbook with somebody. Would you write one with me?"

I said, "We ought to be a great team. You can't write and I'm not supposed to be able to, so let's do it!"

Thus began this great career of writing and teaching. We wrote a textbook called *Management of Organizational Behavior: Utilizing Human Resources*. It came out in its eighth edition October 3, 2000 and the nineth edition will be out June 15, 2007. It has sold more than any other textbook in that area over the years. It's been over forty years since that book came out.

I quit my administrative job, became a professor, and ended up working my way up the ranks. I got a sabbatical leave and went to California for one year twenty-five years ago. I ended up meeting Spencer Johnson at a cocktail party. He wrote children's books—a wonderful series called *Value Tales for Kids including*. He also wrote *The Value of Courage: The Story of Jackie Robinson and The Value of Believing In Yourself: The Story Louis Pasteur*.

My wife, Margie, met him first and said, "You guys ought to write a children's book for managers because they won't read anything else." That was my introduction to Spencer. So, *The One Minute Manager* was really a kid's book for big people. That is a long way from saying that my career was well planned.

Wright

Ken, what and/or who were your early influences in the areas of business, leadership and success? In other words, who shaped you in your early years?

Blanchard

My father had a great impact on me. He was retired as an admiral in the Navy and had a wonderful philosophy. I remember when I was elected as president of the seventh grade, and I came home all pumped up. My father said, "Son, it's great that you're the president of the seventh grade, but now that you have that leadership position, don't ever use it." He said, "Great leaders are followed because people respect them and like them, not because they have power." That was a wonderful lesson for me early on. He was just a great model for me. I got a lot from him.

Then I had this wonderful opportunity in the mid 1980s to write a book with Norman Vincent Peale. He wrote *The Power of Positive Thinking*. I met him when he was eighty-six years old and we were asked to write a book on ethics together, *The Power of Ethical Management: Integrity Pays, You Don't Have to Cheat to Win*. It didn't matter what we were writing together, I learned so much from him, and he just built from the positive things I learned from my mother.

My mother said that when I was born I laughed before I cried, I danced before I walked, and I smiled before I frowned. So that, as well as Norman Vincent Peale, really impacted me as I focused on what I could do to train leaders. How do you make them positive? How do you make them realize that it's not about them, it's about who they are serving. It's not about their position, it's about what they can do to help other people win.

So, I'd say my mother and father, then Norman Vincent Peale, all had a tremendous impact on me.

Wright

I can imagine. I read a summary of your undergraduate and graduate degrees. I assumed you studied business administration, marketing management, and related courses. Instead, at Cornell you studied government and philosophy. You received your master's from Colgate in sociology and counseling and your PhD from Cornell in educational administration and leadership. Why did you choose this course of study? How has it affected your writing and consulting?

Blanchard

Well, again, it wasn't really well planned out. I originally went to Colgate to get a master's degree in education because I was going to be a Dean of Students over men. I had been a government major, and I was a government major because it was the best department at Cornell in the Liberal Arts School. It was exciting. We would study what the people were doing at the league governments. And then, the Philosophy Department was great. I just loved the philosophical arguments. I wasn't a great student in terms of getting grades, but I'm a total learner. I would sit there and listen, and I would really soak it in.

When I went over to Colgate and got in these education courses, they were awful. They were boring. The second week, I was sitting at the bar at the Colgate Inn saying, "I can't believe I've been here two years for this." It's just the way the Lord works—sitting next to me in the bar was a young sociology professor who had just gotten his PhD at Illinois. He was staying at the Inn. I was moaning and groaning about what I was doing, and he said, "Why don't you come and major with me in sociology? It's really exciting."

"I can do that?" I asked.

He said, "Yes."

I knew they would probably let me do whatever I wanted the first week. Suddenly, I switched out of education and went with Warren Ramshaw. He had a tremendous impact on me. He retired some years ago as the leading professor at Colgate in the Arts and Sciences, and got me interested in leadership and organizations. That's why I got a master's in sociology.

The reason I went into educational administration and leadership? It was a doctoral program I could get into because I knew the guy heading up the program. He said, "The greatest thing about Cornell is that you will be in a School of Education. It's not very big, so you don't have to take many education courses, and you can take stuff all over the place."

There was a marvelous man by the name of Don McCarty, who eventually became the Dean of the School of Education, Wisconsin. He had an impact on my life; but I was always just searching around. My mission statement is: to be a loving teacher and example of simple truths that help myself and others to awaken the presence of God in our lives. The reason I mention "God" is that I believe the biggest addiction in the world is the human ego; but I'm really into simple truth. I used to tell people I was trying to get the B.S. out of the behavioral sciences.

Wright

I can't help but think, when you mentioned your father, that he just bottomed lined it for you about leadership.

Blanchard

Yes.

Wright

A man named Paul Myers, in Texas, years and years ago when I went to a conference down there, said, "David, if you think you're a leader and you look around, and no one is following you, you're just out for a walk."

Blanchard

Well, you'd get a kick; I'm just reaching over to pick up a picture of Paul Myers on my desk. He's a good friend, and he's a part of our Center for FaithWalk Leadership where we're trying to challenge and equip people to lead like Jesus. It's non-profit. I tell people I'm not an evangelist because we've got enough trouble with the Christians we have. We don't need any more new ones. But, this is a picture of Paul on top of a mountain. Then there's another picture below that of him under the sea with stingrays. It says, "Attitude is everything. Whether you're on the top of the mountain or the bottom of the sea, true happiness is achieved by accepting God's promises, and by having a biblically positive frame of mind. Your attitude is everything." Isn't that something?

Wright

He's a fine, fine man. He helped me tremendously. In keeping with the theme of our book, *Speaking of Success,* I wanted to get a sense from you about your own success journey. Many people know you best from *The One Minute Manager* books you coauthored with Spencer Johnson. Would you consider these books as a high water mark for you, or have you defined success for yourself in different terms?

Blanchard

Well, you know, *The One Minute Manager* was an absurdly successful book, so quickly that I found I couldn't take credit for it. That was when I really got on my own spiritual journey and started to try to find out what the real meaning of life and success was.

That's been a wonderful journey for me because I think, David, the problem with most people is they think their self-worth is a function of their performance plus the opinion of others. The minute you think that is what your self-worth is, every day your self-worth is up for grabs because your performance is going to fluctuate on a day-to-day basis. People are fickle. Their opinions are going to go up and down. You need to ground your self-worth in the unconditional love that

God has ready for us, and that really grew out of the unbelievable success of *The One Minute Manager.*

When I started to realize where all that came from, that's how I got involved in this ministry that I mentioned. Paul Myers is a part of it. As I started to read the Bible, I realized that everything I've ever written about, or taught, Jesus did. You know, He did it with the twelve incompetent guys He "hired." The only guy with much education was Judas, and he was His only turnover problem.

Wright

Right.

Blanchard

It was a really interesting thing. What I see in people is not only do they think their self-worth is a function of their performance plus the opinion of others, but they measure their success on the amount of accumulation of wealth, on recognition, power, and status. I think those are nice success items. There's nothing wrong with those, as long as you don't define your life by that.

What I think you need to focus on rather than success is what Bob Buford, in his book *Halftime,* calls significance—moving from success to significance. I think the opposite of accumulation of wealth is generosity.

I wrote a book called *The Generosity Factor* with Truett Cathy, who is the founder of Chick-fil-A. He is one of the most generous men I've ever met in my life. I thought we needed to have a model of generosity. It's not only your treasure, but it's your time and talent. Truett and I added *touch* as a fourth one.

The opposite of recognition is service. I think you become an adult when you realize you're here to serve rather than to be served.

Finally, the opposite of power and status is loving relationships. Take Mother Teresa as an example; she couldn't have cared less about recognition, power, and status because she was focused on generosity, service, and loving relationships; but she got all of that earthly stuff. If you focus on the earthly, such as money, recognition, and power, you're never going to get to significance. But if you focus on significance, you'll be amazed at how much success can come your way.

Wright

I spoke with Truett Cathy recently and was impressed by what a down-to-earth, good man he seems to be. When you start talking about him closing on Sunday, all of my friends—when they found out I had talked to him—said, "Boy, he must be a great Christian man, but he's rich and all this." I told them, "Well, to put his faith into perspective, by closing on Sunday it cost him $500 million a year."

He lives his faith, doesn't he?

Blanchard

Absolutely, but he still outsells everybody else.

Wright

That's right.

Blanchard

According to their January 25, 2007, press release, Chick-fil-A is currently the nation's second-largest quick-service chicken restaurant chain in sales. Its business performance marks the thirty-ninth consecutive year the chain has enjoyed a system-wide sales gain—a streak the company has sustained since opening its first chain restaurant in 1967.

Wright

The simplest market scheme, I told him, tripped me up. I walked by his first Chick-fil-A I had ever seen, and some girl came out with chicken stuck on toothpicks and handed me one; I just grabbed it and ate it, it's history from there on.

Blanchard

Yes, I think so. It's really special. It is so important that people understand generosity, service, and loving relationships because too many people are running around like a bunch of peacocks. You even see pastors who measure their success by how many in are in their congregation; authors by how many books they have sold; businesspeople by what their profit margin is—how good sales are. The reality is that's all well and good, but I think what you need to focus on is the other. I think if business did that more and we got Wall Street off our backs with all the short-term evaluation, we'd be a lot better off.

Wright

Absolutely. There seems to be a clear theme that winds through many of your books that have to do with success in business and organizations—how people are treated by management and how they feel about their value to a company. Is this an accurate observation? If so, can you elaborate on it?

Blanchard

Yes, it's a very accurate observation. See, I think the profit is the applause you get for taking care of your customers and creating a motivating environment for your people. Very often people think that business is only about the bottom line. But no, that happens to be the result of creating raving fan customers, which I've described with Sheldon Bowles in our book, *Raving Fans*. Customers want to brag about you, if you create an environment where people can be gung-ho and committed. You've got to take care of your customers and your people, and then your cash register is going to go ka-ching, and you can make some big bucks.

Wright

I noticed that your professional title with the Ken Blanchard Companies is somewhat unique—Chairman and Chief Spiritual Officer. What does your title mean to you personally and to your company? How does it affect the books you choose to write?

Blanchard

I remember having lunch with Max DuPree one time, the legendary Chairman of Herman Miller, who wrote a wonderful book called *Leadership Is An Art.* "What's your job?" I asked him.

He said, "I basically work in the vision area."

"Well, what do you do?" I asked.

"I'm like a third grade teacher," he replied. "I say our vision and values over, and over, and over again until people get it right, right, right."

I decided from that, I was going to become the Chief Spiritual Officer, which means I would be working in the vision, values, and energy part of our business. I ended up leaving a morning message every day for everybody in our company. We have twenty-eight international offices around the world. I leave a voice mail every morning, and I do three things on that as Chief Spiritual Officer: One, people tell me who we need to pray for. Two, people tell me who we need to praise—

our unsung heroes and people like that. And then three, I leave an inspirational morning message. I really am the cheerleader—the Energizer Bunny—in our company. I'm the reminder of why we're here and what we're trying to do.

We think that our business in the Ken Blanchard Companies is to help people lead at a higher level, and to help individuals and organizations. Our mission statement is to unleash the power and potential of people and organizations for the common good. So if we are going to do that, we've really got to believe in that.

I'm working on getting more Chief Spiritual Officers around the country. I think it's a great title and we should get more of them.

Wright

So those people for whom you pray, where do you get the names?

Blanchard

The people in the company tell me who needs help, whether it's a spouse who is sick, or kids who are sick, or they are worried about something. We've got over five years of data about the power of prayer, which is pretty important.

One morning, my inspirational message was about my wife and five members of our company who walked sixty miles one weekend—twenty miles a day for three days—to raise money for breast cancer research.

It was amazing. I went down and waved them all in as they came. They had a ceremony, and they had raised 7.6 million dollars. There were over three thousand people walking, and a lot of the walkers were dressed in pink; they were cancer victors—people who had overcome it. There were even men walking with pictures of their wives who had died from breast cancer. I thought it was incredible.

There wasn't one mention about it in the major San Diego papers. I said, "Isn't that just something." We have to be an island of positive influence because all you see in the paper today is about Michael Jackson and Scott Peterson and Kobe Bryant—celebrities and their bad behavior—and here you get all these thousands of people out there walking and trying to make a difference, and nobody thinks it's news.

So every morning I pump people up about what life's about, about what's going on. That's what my Chief Spiritual Officer job is about.

Wright

I had the pleasure of reading one of your releases, *The Leadership Pill.*

Blanchard

Yes.

Wright

I must admit that my first thought was how short the book was. I wondered if I was going to get my money's worth, which by the way, I most certainly did. Many of your books are brief and based on a fictitious story. Most business books in the market today are hundreds of pages in length and are read almost like a textbook.

Will you talk a little bit about why you write these short books, and about the premise of *The Leadership Pill?*

Blanchard

I really developed my relationship with Spencer Johnson when we wrote *The One Minute Manager.* As you know, he wrote, *Who Moved My Cheese,* which was a phenomenal success. He wrote children's books, and is quite a storyteller.

Jesus taught by parables, which were short stories.

My favorite books are, *Jonathan Livingston Seagull* and *The Little Prince.*

Og Mandino, author of seventeen books, was the greatest of them all.

I started writing parables because people can get into the story and learn the contents of the story, and they don't bring their judgmental hats into reading. You write a regular book and they'll say, "Well, where did you get the research?" They get into that judgmental side. Our books get them emotionally involved and they learn.

The Leadership Pill is a fun story about a pharmaceutical company who thinks that they have discovered the secret to leadership, and they can put the ingredients in a pill. When they announce it, the country goes crazy because everybody knows we need more effective leaders. When they release it, it outsells Viagra. The founders of the company start selling off stock and they call them Pillionaires. But along comes this guy who calls himself "the effective manager," and he challenges them to a no-pill challenge. If they identify two non-performing groups, he'll take on one and let somebody on the pill take another one, and he guarantees he will out-perform that person by the end of the year. They agree, but of course they give him a drug test every week to make sure he's not sneaking pills on the side.

I wrote the book with Marc Muchnick, who is a young guy in his early thirties. We did a major study of what this interesting "Y" generation, the young people of today, want from leaders, and this is a secret blend that this effective manager uses. When you think about it, David, it is really powerful on terms of what people want from a leader.

Number one, they want integrity. A lot of people have talked about that in the past, but these young people will walk if they see people say one thing and do another. A lot of us walk to the bathroom and out into the halls to talk about it. But these people will quit. They don't want somebody to say something and not do it.

The second thing they want is a partnership relationship. They hate superior/subordinate. I mean, what awful terms those are. You know, the "head" of the department and the hired "hands"—you don't even give them a head. "What do you do? I'm in supervision. I see things a lot clearer than these stupid idiots." They want to be treated as partners; if they can get a financial partnership, great. If they can't, they really want a minimum of psychological partnership where they can bring their brains to work and make decisions.

Then finally, they want affirmation. They not only want to be caught doing things right, but they want to be affirmed for who they are. They want to be known as a person, not as a number.

So those are the three ingredients that this effective manager uses. They are wonderful values when you think about them.

Rank-order values for any organization is number one, integrity. In our company we call it ethics. It is our number one value. The number two value is partnership. In our company we call it relationships. Number three is affirmation—being affirmed as a human being. I think that ties into relationships, too. They are wonderful values that can drive behavior in a great way.

Wright

I believe most people in today's business culture would agree that success in business has everything to do with successful leadership. In *The Leadership Pill*, you present a simple but profound premise, that leadership is not something you do to people, it's something you do *with* them. At face value, that seems incredibly obvious. But you must have found in your research and observations that leaders in today's culture do not get this. Would you speak to that issue?

Blanchard

Yes. I think what often happens in this is the human ego. There are too many leaders out there who are self-serving. They're not leaders who have service in mind. They think the sheep are there for the benefit of the shepherd. All the power, money, fame, and recognition moves up the hierarchy; they forget that the real action in business is not up the hierarchy; it's in the one-to-one, moment-to-moment interactions that your front line people have with your customers. It's how the phone is answered. It's how problems are dealt with and those kinds of things. If you don't think that you're doing leadership *with* them—rather, you're doing it to them—after a while they won't take care of your customers.

I was at a store once (not Nordstrom's, where I normally would go) and I thought of something I had to share with my wife, Margie. I asked the guy behind the counter in Men's Wear, "May I use your phone?"

He said, "No!"

"You're kidding me," I said. "I can always use the phone at Nordstrom's."

"Look, buddy," he said, "they won't let *me* use the phone here. Why should I let you use the phone?"

That is an example of leadership that's done *to* employees not *with* them. People want a partnership. People want to be involved in a way that really makes a difference.

Wright

Dr. Blanchard, the time has flown by and there are so many more questions I'd like to ask you. In closing, would you mind sharing with our readers some thoughts on success? If you were mentoring a small group of men and women, and one of their central goals was to become successful, what kind of advice would you give them?

Blanchard

Well, I would first of all say, "What are you focused on?" If you are focused on success as being, as I said earlier, accumulation of money, recognition, power, or status, I think you've got the wrong target. What you need to really be focused on is how you can be generous in the use of your time and your talent and your treasure and touch. How can you serve people rather than be served? How can you develop caring, loving relationships with people? My sense is if you will focus on those things, success in the traditional sense will come to you. But if you go out and say, "Man, I'm going to make a fortune, and I'm going to do this," and have that kind of attitude, you might get some of those numbers. I think you become an adult, however, when you realize you are here to give rather than to get. You're here to serve not to be served. I would just say to people, "Life is such a very special occasion. Don't miss it by aiming at a target that bypasses other people, because we're really here to serve each other." So that's what I would share with people.

Wright

Well, what an enlightening conversation, Dr. Blanchard. I really want you to know how much I appreciate all the time you've taken with me for this interview. I know that our readers will learn from this, and I really appreciate your being with us today.

Blanchard

Well, thank you so much, David. I really enjoyed my time with you. You've asked some great questions that made me think, and I hope my answers are helpful to other people because as I say, life is a special occasion.

Wright

Today we have been talking with Dr. Ken Blanchard. He is the author of the phenomenal best selling book, *The One Minute Manager*. The fact that he's the Chief Spiritual Officer of his company should make us all think about how we are leading our companies and leading our families and leading anything, whether it is in church or civic organizations. I know I will.

Thank you so much, Dr. Blanchard, for being with us today on *Speaking of Success.*

Blanchard

Good to be with you, David.

About The Author

Few people have created more of a positive impact on the day-to-day management of people and companies than Dr. Kenneth Blanchard, who is known around the world simply as "Ken."

When Ken speaks, he speaks from the heart with warmth and humor. His unique gift is to speak to an audience and communicate with each individual as if they were alone and talking one-on-one. He is a polished storyteller with a knack for making the seemingly complex easy to understand.

Ken has been a guest on a number of national television programs, including *Good Morning America* and *The Today Show*. He has been featured in *Time, People, U.S. News* & *World Report*, and a host of other popular publications.

He earned his bachelor's degree in government and philosophy from Cornell University, his master's degree in sociology and counseling from Colgate University, and his PhD in educational administration and leadership from Cornell University.

Dr. Ken Blanchard
The Ken Blanchard Companies
125 State Place
Escondido, California 92029
Phone: 800.728.6000
Fax: 760.489.8407
www.kenblanchard.com

Chapter 4

JENNIFER POWERS

THE INTERVIEW

David Wright (Wright)

Jennifer Powers is a highly successful coach, speaker, and facilitator who has made it her life's work to help people uncover their own qualities for success. She is a leading expert in providing personal development for professional growth to entrepreneurs, professionals, and organizations that are ready to shift into action. Jennifer is a graduate of University of Delaware and earned her master's degree in Sociology from the University of Houston. She serves on the Board of the Northwest Coaches Association and is an active member of the National Speakers Association. The energy and excitement Jennifer brings to her line of work is contagious as she inspires changes in the lives and businesses of her clients across the country. Jennifer's belief system is simple—life doesn't have to be anything less than amazing—and she is passionate about sharing that message with the world.

Jennifer, welcome to *Speaking of Success.*

Jennifer Powers (Powers)

Thank you, David.

Wright

Jennifer, I know you've heard many, many definitions of success, but how do you define success?

Powers

Well, I am certain that there are as many definitions of success as there are people to define it. Success is a personal journey. It's an evolution that continues throughout our lives, so each individual's definition of success will be ever-changing.

As you age and enter into different phases of your life, your priorities and objectives change as will your definition of success. Allowing this process to take its course is an awesome thing.

So at this moment, my personal definition of success is living your most authentic life. What I mean by "authentic" is honoring what feels right on a daily basis and acting on those feelings. That to me is success. If, at the end of the day I am feeling ("feeling" being the operative word here) positive about the choices I made, the work I did, and the people I interacted with, *and* I look forward to waking up and doing more of it the next day, then I have achieved success. Now, ask me again in ten years and I might give you a completely different answer! But one thing I know for sure is that I will define my success in terms of my feelings as much then as I do now.

Feelings are not always considered when defining success because that is not the type of culture we live in. Traditional tools of measurement are wealth, education, dress size, material possessions, and the answer to the infamous question, "So, what do you do?" among other things. However, it is exciting to me that every day more and more people are defining and honoring what they truly want out of life and are disregarding what the societal norms dictate. And when they discover that achieving success is as simple as honoring their feelings, then they will have arrived. I invite people to consider the possibility that by simply following their feelings they can pave their way to success.

Wright

That is very interesting. Will you talk a bit more about how people can use their feelings to achieve success?

Powers

Sure, I think the best way is to compare it to shopping for a pair of shoes. Some shoes you try on might look great—they may be designer shoes or attractively priced. You may walk around in them comfortably for a short time but after a while they start to feel uncomfortable. Certain spots are rubbing you in the wrong way and you begin to realize that although they may have looked good originally, they may not be such a good fit after all.

If something in your life feels incongruent, then it is time to check in with whether or not what you are doing is a good fit. Sometimes we get involved in careers, businesses, relationships, etc., thinking it would or could or even *should* feel right, but it's not until you are in it for some length of time that you realize it is not meeting your authentic needs and, therefore, you are unable to experience success.

For example, there was a time when I thought success meant working for a large corporation in a corner office with a huge salary, 401(k), and benefits package. So, I worked hard to find a job just like that. I got it and I thought for sure I had "arrived." I was going to be rolling around in money and benefits, and retirement would be great. And yes, I could have rolled around in it and basked in the light of success. But it wasn't *my* success. I was unhappy and terribly unfulfilled.

So, if something doesn't resonate with you as you thought it would, that's okay! The sooner you recognize that feeling of discomfort and honor it, the more direct your path to success will be. But you must give it the attention it deserves and do it tenaciously. You must move on to consider other possibilities. For the sake of our metaphor, you must continue to try on shoes until you find "the pair" that fits! This can be applied to any and all facets of your life.

Think for a moment about your relationships, eating habits, self-care, career track, or parenting. Check in with the way you "feel" about each of those areas and use this feeling to get clarity around what you need to change in your life. When you know what is off kilter you are better prepared to make the necessary choices for success.

For example, if you are told jogging is the best way to stay in shape, but the thought of actually doing it turns your stomach, don't force it. Disregard what the experts are saying you need to do to be fit. If it doesn't feel right to you then it's not going to work! So, honor that feeling and move on to find an activity that feels better. If you do, you are more likely to follow through with your plan to perform that activity on a consistent basis. Success!

Same thing goes for relationships. How many people are spending their lives with a spouse or partner who isn't a good fit for them? Why do they continue with the struggle of trying to make it work? Living an authentic life helps you to avoid situations like that because when you are authentic you honor what feels right on a daily basis and you act on those feelings.

Mind you, success does not come without some sacrifice. Leaving a spouse or partner is difficult, but what I invite you to do when a struggle like this presents itself is to take a thirty-thousand-foot view of the situation and understand that in order to have success in the future you must honor your feelings in the present, no matter how difficult it seems.

At the end of the day, if you stay true to who you are and follow what feels right, you will experience less struggle, less heartache, and less confusion. Answers and decisions will come to you with ease and you will have a sense of freedom, endless possibility, and enormous potential. I have lived it and I coach people toward this on a daily basis. It is truly empowering.

Wright

How have you used this tactic on your own journey toward success and what would you say would be the greatest contribution to your own success?

Powers

I have both learned and applied this tactic on my journey and I am still learning! Being patient and giving myself the permission and the space to find my authentic path was key. I searched relentlessly for the professional path that felt true to me. I knew that if it felt true, success would be a natural consequence, and guess what? I was right! Absolute empowerment comes from considering all of your possibilities.

If it means trying on every shoe in the shop, then that's what should happen. And believe me, I've tried on *many* different shoes. But I never gave up and I never tired. I knew I had to keep going, searching, believing, and knowing that I would eventually arrive. And finally, I got that feeling and I literally yelled, "Eureka!" Things finally felt congruent and authentic. I had found a way to combine my true wants with my true talents and I hit pay dirt!

So now, when I coach my clients to live their most authentic life, I ask them what they really, really want and who they really, really are. It is the combination of these two things that we all need to tap into. If we honor what we most desire and we use the best of who we are to get it, we have a fail-proof recipe for success.

And so, I think the greatest contributions to my success are my willingness to trust in the process and honor my needs along the way.

I remind myself to not only trust the process, but to enjoy the journey almost on a daily basis and I do so whether I experience negativity or positivity because that, like anything, is where we find the balance.

So if there is a day when things aren't going exactly as I planned, I find peace, reason, and sense in that because I know it is part of the process. Boy, the day I discovered that one simple truth it really turned my perspective around. I began to feel more in control and less like a victim of circumstance.

And the second part of that is continuing to honor my needs, even as they change. What seems good today might seem mediocre tomorrow and that's perfectly normal. I have learned that patience isn't only a virtue but a coping mechanism. The more gentle we are with ourselves, the more open we are to receiving the answers we're looking for.

In the end, being successful is about being your best self in the best place at this very moment. It sounds simple, and it is. It's just not always easy.

Wright

What do you think are the biggest obstacles people face in trying to become successful?

Powers

That's a great question. Actually, I believe that you can't have success without obstacles. These so called "obstacles" are part of the journey toward success because in order to have peaks you must have valleys. It is a natural truth that will forever remain the same.

So I like to think of obstacles as opportunities because when we find ourselves in the valleys we are given an opportunity to regroup and perhaps re-chart our course to the peak. It is when we are down that we are most vulnerable, but we are also the most motivated to effect change.

If people tell me they are running into a lot of obstacles, I invite them to change the way they look at the obstacle and ask how they could use it to propel themselves to the next level, to learn from it, to become stronger, etc.

So to answer your question, I believe the only obstacle standing in the way of a person's success is perspective. Too often we use small bumps in the road as an excuse for not moving forward and soon enough we are making that bump into a mountain that is now clearly standing in the way of our success.

Wayne Dyer reminds us that, "If you change the way you look at things, the things you look at change." What a great truth! How different would life be if we all looked at our challenges and hardships as opportunities for growth, renewal, and success? Now *that* is what I call making the most of every aspect of life.

Wright

So, is perspective enough or is it only a facet of a person's journey to success? What do you think is really necessary for people to, as you say, close the gap between where they are and where they want to be?

Powers

Well, I am glad you asked because although perspective plays a big part in handling obstacles along the way there is definitely more to it than that. I have learned that there are three important steps to closing that gap: you've got to walk, talk, and stalk success.

The first step is to *walk* in the space where your authentic self lives and thrives. When you find those comfy shoes, walk in them! Let yourself be who you are. Doing so allows your greatest strengths and talents to come out and work in your favor. Trust that living your authentic life and honoring who you are will result in your getting where you want to go.

We all have special talents, skills, and abilities that are unique to us but equally important to the world. I believe that if we can tap into our own natural resources, we can achieve greatness.

On the other hand, if we try to fight nature by trying to be comfy in a shoe that doesn't fit, we are eluding success. We can try to act successful but we will never really arrive because we are not in our best suited role, job, relationship, or whatever. It would be like trying to run a marathon in a pair of stilettos.

Second, you have to *talk* success. So many of us forget that we can use the power of words to create our reality. Once you decide where you want to go, speak "as if" you have already arrived. Tell yourself you are a success every day. Look in the mirror and say out loud. "I am a wildly successful person!" Believe me, it works.

One of my favorite lines comes from a popular eighties movie: "If you can't say it, you can't do it." If you are not using the power of words to support you on your journey to success, you are taking the long way home. By simply saying out loud that which you want to achieve or be, you are one step closer to making it a reality. If you can't say it then you probably don't believe it, and if you don't believe it why should anyone else?

Many people throughout history have proven that it's possible to literally talk your way to success.

Mohammed Ali shocked the public with his outrageous behavior and self-promotion saying, "I am the greatest!" Yet what people failed to realize was that this high level of positive self-talk and thinking was, in part, what led him to victory. By saying it, he believed it, and so others believed it and *bingo!* he became the greatest fighter of his time.

In the early eighties when Dick Clark asked a virtually unknown guest singer on American Bandstand what she would like to do twenty years from now, she confidently answered, "To rule the world." And that's exactly what Madonna did.

It is amazing how few of us practice that simple task and how very powerful it is when we do.

Finally, you have to *stalk* success. This is a no-brainer. You have to be a tenacious lion. Be relentless in your pursuit and go after what you want with reckless abandon. I have learned that when the going gets tough, I have to be tougher. I know that is easier said than done, but if it were easy everyone would be doing it.

Figure out what you intend to accomplish in your life, then go in for the kill. Let your animal instinct kick in and claim what's yours. Set out to live a bigger life. Explore new horizons! Consider the possibilities and venture fearlessly toward those you want to experience.

So, here's the thing: doing any one of the above will get you moving in the right direction, but if you really want to close the gap between where you are and where you want to be you have to apply all three steps *simultaneously* and consistently.

This is the one of the best reasons to hire a coach. It is not easy to do it alone and you shouldn't have to. A coach can and will keep you on track in all three of these areas so that you can arrive in half the time and with fewer bruises!

Wright

In your opinion, what's the one quality all successful people have?

Powers

Successful people understand that their reality is not a result of extraneous circumstances, but a result of the collective choices they make. They recognize and exercise their power of choice and they never hold anyone but themselves accountable for what happens in their lives.

Successful people submit to the fact that life doesn't have to be anything less than amazing. They never settle. Their tenacity and commitment to success drives them toward stepping into a greatness bigger than themselves. They think big and so they *are* big.

Too many people believe that life is about compromises. They tell themselves they can't have all that they want so they make sacrifices and find excuses for not living a fully satisfying life. I say "No! No way." I don't buy that and neither should anyone else. It is our natural birthright to pursue happiness and success however we define it. So, what all successful people have in common is a belief in their own power to win and a conviction to choose success over anything else.

I know that if I want to be successful in anything I have to believe it is within my reach. Henry Ford once said, "Whether you think you can or think you can't, you're right."

You are what you choose to be so why not choose to be a screaming success?

Wright

Would you tell our readers a little bit about what drives you to be successful?

Powers

Personally, what drives me to be successful is the opportunity to impact other people's success. To be in service to people and know that I am playing a part, big or small, in their progress keeps me going strong. I believe in people's ability to be great and it is my life's work and mission to help individuals "arrive." When they win I win.

I want to witness as many people as possible step into greatness once and for all. It goes back to the *feeling* I spoke about earlier. Helping people achieve their own success is what feels right for me and so I look for ways to do that more and more every day.

I can't think of anything more exciting than contributing to and promoting other peoples' dreams. I work with a lot of small business owners and entrepreneurs who have these big visions with a roaring fire in their belly and I get so much energy from them. Fueling that fire is what I love to do.

Actually, this is something we can all experience on one level or another. You don't have to be a coach, speaker, or consultant to find success in helping others. There is so much gratification from being in service and giving back. Again, this is no big secret, but how many of us are practicing that in our business circles? We are taught that in order to win we have to be the one with the most toys. But times are changing and many people are becoming wise to the fact that generosity breeds prosperity.

It's a new day and the me-first capitalist could be taking the back seat to the leaders who are finding a way for everyone to win. Freely sharing knowledge and compassion to benefit others is what I strive to do. Now, this isn't necessarily new in the business world. Our culture has embraced that philosophy in the past, and there are still those who are in tune with it today, but certainly not the majority.

This is what drives me to be successful—helping people win. I would do it if I weren't a coach but that is the beauty of it, I get paid for something I love doing, so I feel very fortunate.

Wright

As a coach, how do you help people achieve success?

Powers

Well, first I start by challenging people to consider all their possibilities so they can come full circle to where they need to be. Working very closely with each client, I get them to recognize the enormous potential they have inside of them. They say that the four most powerful words in the English language are "I believe in you." I love, love, love telling my clients that and they love hearing it. We humans need to hear that.

Second, I push my clients to stretch their goals beyond what they think they can accomplish—way beyond! People are always so appreciative of that because we have a tendency to place limitations on ourselves and as a result we experience frustration for not achieving enough. I encourage you to try it. The next time you set a goal, ask yourself, "Is that big enough?" In order to *be* big we've got to *think* big. The more we can stretch our goals the more we empower ourselves to reach them.

Third, and probably the most powerful, is I help my clients use what they have to get what they want. By that I mean we work together to define what unique talents and characteristics they have that make them great. Once we do that we focus on those characteristics and recognize them as their absolute assets.

One of my favorite truths in life and words I love to live by are: What you focus on will grow! Like attracts like. It's a universal law. So if we focus on all of the things we do well that bring us success, we will attract more success. We need to believe that what we have inside of us is all we need to step into greatness. Believe it, focus on it, and let it take you where you want to go.

Wright

That makes a lot of sense, Jennifer. Tell me more about what makes your approach unique?

Powers

Well, most importantly, I don't pretend to provide people with quick-fix answers and solutions to their problems. Instead, I tell them that it will take a substantial amount of inner and outer work on their part. What I offer people is the opportunity to consider their own possibility, to tap into their best self, and use that to get where they want to go. We all have the answers inside of us but we have to understand that my answers will be different than your answers so there is no cookie-cutter solution.

I provide the tools, resources, and guidance for people to reach deep down within themselves to find their own truths and talents and ultimately their own individual path to success.

Success is highly personal so my approach is as unique as each individual I work with. Therefore, the approach is not always the same—it's wide open. Possibilities abound and I love that!

Allowing people to come up with their own solutions is empowering and it will always stand the test of time. I don't try to motivate people to greatness but instead, help them identify their own compass to lead them there.

Wright

How do you use this approach to benefit the corporate world?

Powers

I apply the same coaching technique in a group setting with a proprietary program called "Breakthrough Thinking." The objective is to offer entire teams the space to be heard and feel empowered, first as individuals and then as part of a very cohesive team. As a result, they feel enabled and eager to make a difference.

Helping team members discover their authentic selves and tap into their talents will benefit them on a *personal* level and the organization on a *business* level. This is very powerful and highly effective.

Organizations must realize there is great value in their employees. Everyone has something very special and unique to offer and it is my mission to help individuals find those qualities within themselves and apply them in ways that will benefit the company. The employees feel empowered and the company excels—it's a win-win!

Many times my corporate clients are amazed by someone in whom they saw little potential come up with incredible ideas and solutions once they are given the space to express themselves and be who they are. If you just give people permission to be their best selves it's amazing what can happen.

There is room for this at the corporate level and what's more, there is a huge calling for it right now. This must happen if an organization wants to stay ahead. The nature of today's workplace has stifled creativity and individualism to an absolute fault and it's time for change.

It goes back to the belief that what you focus on will grow. If you want to generate more of anything, you must give it more attention. So if you want your team to be more creative in their problem-solving, give them space to do so. Withholding that opportunity will have the opposite effect and I think many companies are starting to realize that.

I tell every business leader I work with that the answer to the problem he or she is having is not going to come from me. It's going to come from the people within the organization. They have the answers; I draw them out.

Through my program I help people focus on their brilliance to create more of it and to ultimately support the company's mission. This has never failed to blow people away. It is an awesome process.

Wright

So how do you foresee the union of inspiration and corporation developing in the future?

Powers

I think it is going to go back to the basics. Businesses and organizations are starting to realize that it is not only about what they want out of an employee but what the employee wants out of them.

Unlike our recent past when loyalty to the company kept people around, employers need to be more creative. They need to respond to the needs of their staff to not only keep them from looking elsewhere, but to keep them engaged and motivated to support the mission of the organization.

So what I envision is employers starting to invest in the interests of their people and in doing so they are going to get back a bigger ROI than they ever imagined. Here's why: when you show an interest in supporting the personal development of an individual, you not only get a more loyal employee, you get a more motivated employee and with that comes increased productivity, morale and, of course, profit.

See, if you want to invest in the organization, you need not look further than the employee. Inspire employees and believe in them. Communicate that belief in them. Give them space to be heard. People respond to being heard and that feels good. When you have a group of employees who are all feeling good, you get a stronger, more competitive edge in your market. It is not rocket science.

My personal mission, and that of my business, is to lead organizations down this path and facilitate them in empowering their people to be all they can be . . . not only for the sake of the company but for the "feeling" of the individuals. See, it all comes full circle.

Wright

What is the message you want people to hear so they can learn from your success?

Powers

Oh! But there are so many messages, where do I start?

Okay, how about giving you my top ten list? I carry this with me wherever I go and refer to it often as a reminder of all I've learned so far.

1. Think big. Believe you can and then some! Whatever you can envision achieving, multiply that by five because you have at least that much potential in you.
2. Listen to your gut. Your feelings will always lead you to *your* success.
3. Reach out to others. You are not meant to do this alone. Collaboration and a strong network of supportive people have helped me in more ways than I can count.
4. Know who you are and do what you want. And don't deviate from that, not even for money. (If lost, refer to number two.)
5. Exercise tenacity, tenacity, and more tenacity.
6. Expect and embrace challenges. They will be there whether you welcome them or not.
7. Enjoy the ride. If it takes you your whole life to figure out your path, then die trying because the journey is the best part!
8. Ask for what you want. How can the world conspire to give you what you want if you don't ask for it?
9. Understand that you will not have all the answers—ever.
10. Say yes to success. Give yourself permission to live a bigger life because you truly deserve it.

Wright

What an interesting conversation, Jennifer. I really appreciate your sharing these very insightful thoughts and perspectives on success.

Powers

You're welcome, David. The pleasure is all mine!

About the Author

JENNIFER POWERS is an authority on inspiration and activation. She has made it her life's work to partner with individuals and groups to tap into their unlimited potential and finally close the gap between where they are and where they want to be. Her enthusiastic approach and natural ability to connect with people make her a highly sought-after coach, speaker, and author.

Jennifer combines experience in management, entrepreneurship, and self-discovery with masterful coaching skills to help professionals uncover their own secrets for success. She does this three ways: (1) facilitating her custom designed Breakthrough Thinking Program for business teams, (2) supporting individuals with one-on-one Power Coaching, and (3) delivering highly interactive and inspirational keynotes, workshops, and seminars.

Jennifer earned her master's degree in Sociology from the University of Houston and her coaching certification from the Coach Training Alliance. She is a true believer in the human spirit and is committed to empowering people to find their truths and helping them "arrive."

Jennifer lives and works under the belief that life doesn't have to be anything less than amazing, and she is passionate about sharing that message with the world.

She resides in Salem, Oregon, with her loving husband, Luis, whom she considers to be the real secret to her success.

Jennifer Powers
4676 Commercial St. SE. #83
Salem, OR 97302
Phone: 503.409.0022
Fax: 503.391.6954
E-mail: Jennifer@JenniferPowers.com
www.JenniferPowers.com

Chapter 5

MARTY ZIMMERMAN

THE INTERVIEW

David Wright (Wright)

Today we're talking with Marty Zimmerman. As a top Leadership Development Consultant, Marty individually coached over 1,600 executives and leaders of major industries from all around the world, serving as their leadership performance advisor. The insight he gained from this extensive experience is presented in his book, *In Their Presence: Best Practices and Stories of Role Models.*

He is a U.S. Naval Academy graduate, Marine veteran of twenty-two years, corporate management and executive development consultant, author, and personal coach. He shares what he has learned from leaders' stories of success as related in their personal behaviors as a Visionary and Strategic Thinker.

The question he asks readers most often is, "Do you see yourself in these stories?"

Marty, welcome to *Speaking of Success.*

Marty Zimmerman (Zimmerman)

Thank you, David, I'm glad to be here.

Wright

What is the most important characteristic of a successful business leader?

Zimmerman

Good question—ask ten people and get ten answers—an important question too. I believe demonstrating visionary behaviors is a top characteristic of a successful leader. A dictionary definition of the word "visionary" states "merely speculative and impractical, as an impractical idea. One who has impractical ideas." Recognizing this negative connotation, I offer strategic thinking as an alternative term to visionary. I will share from a different authority on visionary.

Privileged to be coaching global leaders and executives as they receive their leadership performance feedback from their colleagues, I became intrigued by those rated as role model visionary leaders. When asking, "What do you do," I heard the same pattern of responses from this diverse and select people of different languages, industries, and cultures. From them I gained an appreciation for the visionary as a leadership fire that cannot be extinguished. I call it the eternal flame of leadership because the practices of the visionary endure hardship and challenge. The practices of the visionary provide enduring energy for the organization. Visionary practice sheds light on people's thinking and exposes their talents. The enduring success of an organization emerges from this valuable and essential practice.

Wright

What do you mean when you refer to a visionary or strategic thinker?

Zimmerman

I mean a successful leader demonstrates visionary behaviors such as promoting productive conversations and innovative thinking. They promote out-of-the-box thinking that results in increased business. They constructively challenge the status quo thinking in such a way that they prepare us for change. They prepare the people around them to *expect* good things to happen. We can picture some compelling tomorrows, in contrast to today—some future purpose for the organization—and we can communicate its potential and its possibility to others in a universal way where people can see it and they get it.

When people "get it" they can personally see themselves contributing toward that tomorrow. They can visualize contributing to that larger view. This draws out the talents of diverse people. It draws out faith and the ability to take risks and take action, especially when there is uncertainty and ambiguity. It compels people to take risks pursuant to the group's vision, and not pursuant to the emotion of the moment. For example, it might mean giving up one of the best employees as a leader to transfer him or her to another part of the organization, and doing so intentionally, not regretfully.

This practice of the visionary behaviors springboards the emergence of other leadership qualities, and that's what I mean by a "visionary" or strategic thinker.

Wright

What practices do visionary role model leaders demonstrate?

Zimmerman

Ever wonder what it is like to unzip the organization and speak what is normally hidden and never discussed? A role model visionary pattern of practice that has the effect of unzipping the organization is one that asks the same question differently—that's a "how to" I hear visionary leaders around the world indicate when they talk about promoting productive debate and discussion as a behavior. They demonstrate how to ask that same question differently. I'm using that metaphor of unzipping to illustrate that the visionary pattern of practice unzips people from self-imposed restrictions. Recall certain phrases that speak to people's core—phrases that get people in all walks of life to see things differently, no matter what their persuasion. It calls out to them.

Two examples are John F. Kennedy's, "Ask not what your country can do for you, ask what you can do for your country," and Martin Luther King's, "I have a dream . . ." These two visionaries presented a way of unzipping our previously held restrictions and beliefs. They placed us in a position to *act* from a new paradigm and develop a new way of thinking. As I listened to the visionary role model leaders describe their practice of asking the same question differently, I believe this led to their ability to communicate in ways that grabbed people's attention. By asking the same question differently, they invited people to think differently and to consider other possibilities to get from here to there, from today to tomorrow, and to do so with patience and courage.

To me it's the difference between developing an organization that is *leaderless, leader led,* or *leader-full.* I believe an effective measure of a leader's success is the performance of his or her team or organization in his or her absence. Fostering leadership among all challenges the paradigm of too many cooks in the kitchen because the question is not one of labeling everyone as a cook or every employee as a leader, but rather it's expecting everyone to contribute to the workings of a successful kitchen through the eyes of a cook (a leader).

One example of asking the same question differently is when visionaries switch from a "why" question to a "what" question in promoting new thinking, new ideas, or learning. A "why" question usually prompts others to reply with what they already know. While that's useful in some scenarios, this prevents new thinking and possibilities from emerging in conversation. So visionaries unzip the organization's self-imposed restrictions and they unleash people's creative thinking, enabling a future history to be recorded as a result of the habit of asking the same question differently.

Another leader said, "We grew up in the schools, Marty, especially in Western society, conditioned to answering multiple choice—what's the right answer, A, B, C, or D? And the quicker and the more right we were, the better off we were. We got A's, stars, scholarships, and smiley faces on our papers."

Another way one could approach multiple choice questions is to add, "In which situations might A be the better answer? In what circumstances could B or C be right, or when might D be the better solution?" In this way we would be inviting people to *think*—to develop the habit of seeing things differently and developing people's individual capacity to think differently, developing *leader-full* organizations at all levels.

An important distinction here is that the original multiple choice question is a good one. This is not a matter of good or bad, it's a matter of effective and ineffective. In other words, what works for the situation? Situations call for asking the multiple choice question, obviously, to get to the definitive answer so we can move forward. However, for many of us as leaders our routines lull us into this habit of asking the multiple choice question, period. And what differentiates visionaries and makes them successful, according to their employees, is that the employees will also develop the ability to ask the same question differently as a meaningful or productive alternative.

When the people grow, so grows the organization, according to David Wright. Well, this leads to growth and change—it leads to developing new practices, to bridge from here to there. Developing the habit of asking the same question differently sheds light. Like the

Eternal Flame, it continually sheds light onto solutions previously unknown, beyond the original conversation.

In schools teachers can ask a question such as, "With the additional requirements and information, how can I cover all the content in one grading period?" Seeking answers from this very question can actually reinforce the dilemma that educators experience—trying to cover more content. Change the question to, "How can I *uncover* the content in my classroom?" This question can introduce a different path to answers, a new way of looking at the issue, and additional questions. So, "How can I go from covering the content to *uncovering* the content in my classroom?" "How can I shift responsibility for learning from me, the teacher, to my students?" It changes paradigms from a classic, forced-march coverage of the content (teacher talks—students listen) to more of an interactive classroom with the students engaging in the content and sharing their thinking, their confusion, and their comprehension. Students prepare to think their way through tests, not simply regurgitate memorized facts.

Influencing motivation as a leader I might ask myself, "What things can I do or say that motivate others in the workplace?" Asking that question can obviously produce answers. It produces possibilities that in some cases may or may not work, which introduces the power of choice. Asking that same question differently I could also ask, "What things do I do or say or what thoughts do I think, that prevent people around me from feeling motivated?" I now have more possibilities for affecting motivation in the workplace because the first question causes me to look outwardly at how I can influence others, and the second question causes me to look inwardly at what I can control. Both questions are valid, productive, and both questions contribute ways I can impact motivation in my organization.

I learned from visionaries that many of us stop at the first question: "How can I motivate others?" We then move on to the next order of business. Asking the same question differently expands our opportunities, our possibilities, and our tomorrows because it increases seeing what can be. It causes us not to just believe that things can happen, but to expect things to happen. This new way of thinking becomes powerful in our lives. There's an important difference and distinction here.

Questions reveal more possibilities and add clarity to the important decisions, like how to act in conflict especially when emotions are intense. Would I prefer to be right or would I prefer to be effective with this person? What's more important to me at this time?

These are the kinds of insights that visionary leaders provide. When coaching employees, the successful visionary leader often responds to employees' questions with more than just a fast "do it this way" reply. Instead, the visionary leader will respond by asking if some specific solution or another has been tried. For example, "Have you considered trying (this)? Have you thought about doing (that)?" That's characteristic of the visionary leader as coach. Visionary leaders allow employees to make a *choice*. It's not just telling them to follow a set of instructions; rather, it's giving them a choice from which they have the freedom to improvise. This is people development, which is more than sending people to classes. Visionary leaders encourage and exemplify people development at the workplace through their daily interaction with employees. They develop people's habits to decide and improvise, to create, and be committed. The question really becomes, are you developing *leader-full* organizations? As the people grow, so grows the organization.

Wright

What is another useful pattern of habit that visionary role model leaders possess?

Zimmerman

Visionary role model leaders practice a patience and a willingness to encourage people to expand their thinking—"to take a walk in the weeds," "to go out in left field"—to use a couple of colloquialisms. When they brainstorm they seek participants who vary in age, experience, and background to participate if possible. They instinctively rely on a sense of timing on a gut level while the brainstorming occurs. That's what they keep sharing with me. I'm looking for the scientific answers, and they respond with, "It's instinctive."

They can sense when it's time to turn the group from divergent thinking to convergent. One way the visionary accomplishes this is by asking, "What do we now know that we did not know fifteen minutes ago?" It's that patience and that intentional transitioning from the divergent to convergent thinking that I have found to be another pattern of practice among the visionaries.

I first learned this next pattern from a manufacturing plant floor supervisor. His fellow supervisors dismissed the low marks they were receiving in their visionary behaviors by saying, "That's okay; this visionary strategic thinking stuff is for the higher-ups." They felt that their responsibility was only to make decisions, to be operational, to be tactically focused on details.

Then I made a discovery. One of their fellow supervisors, unlike them, was rated as a role model visionary according to his survey results. I asked him, "How is it that you can be rated as a role model with visionary behaviors as a supervisor on the plant floor?" He smiled and replied, "Marty, so many people think that exhibiting visionary leadership is separate from our job here. The visionary behaviors/way of thinking is *a part of, not separate from* the operational or the tactical part of the operation of the business. It supplements and directly supports getting today's work done today."

He then proceeded to share two of his behavior patterns, which again I found to be repetitive among other visionary role models. One was to draw. He said, "People come to my office here with a problem or an issue. They already know to go to my white board, grab a marker, and start drawing out the issue on the board. From this I ask questions like, 'Have you thought about this? If we try this, would that establish precedent? Who else is affected? Who else needs to be involved? Who should we inform right away?' "

As another role model leader has said, "If you can't draw your issues or solutions out, you don't understand them well."

So the visionary encourages a pattern of behavior with the use of drawing to effectively confirm other people's understanding of the issues at all levels of the organization.

And important in my mind is the third pattern of visionaries. They routinely demonstrate the practice of sharing stories and analogies. Stories *breathe*—they breathe purpose, energy, action, focus, and courage into people who face delivering against the odds, even in a hostile environment. Back to the most successful characteristic of leadership and back to my eternal flame analogy, stories reveal and they shed light to the shadows. Stories fundamentally cause people to see something differently and to see other possibilities from which they can choose to take action—possibilities that they otherwise might not have thought possible. And if anticipation is half the joy of realization, stories get us to salivate in anticipation—stories carry across the generations and across cultures, and when we taste we want more!

As an example, one executive credited this analogy, spoken to her by her very first supervisor long ago, for kick-starting her accomplished career. Her supervisor said, "I realize you feel you're being pushed ahead of your time as an expert to the customer, but among little trees, you are a redwood." That analogy shed light on the previous shadow of her own limitations. This executive's story becomes an eternal flame for others because we've all been in our own shadows and can relate. The eternal flame of her story illuminated the courage from which she created her future in response to a compelling vision of herself, not in reaction to how she felt based on the circumstances. Stories and analogies breathe our future into our present. Stories replace a deficit of self-doubt with a surplus of confidence.

Here's another story: One leader's employee had made a wrong decision with good intention at 3:00 AM of a graveyard shift. A client onsite noticed it and sent a complaint up the client leadership chain. Of course, that morning at 8:00 AM this employee's leader receives a chewing out from his client. He turns right around and walks into the annual organizational meeting that begins as scheduled at 8:00 AM, and tells me, "I'm looking at my people; they're quiet and lethargic, and that isn't like them. They knew what had happened and I knew what they were thinking. So I decided to start off the meeting with a question: 'Did anyone ever drive up to a traffic light at three in the morning, just as it turns to red, see no other cars, and even think about running that light?' They began to smile and laugh, as I said, 'Well, I did, and sure enough if there wasn't a cop car in the shadows across the street. It came out and with lights flashing, the cop pulled me over, and gave me a ticket!' "

He continued, "My people knew that had not actually happened, but they got the point." He said he noticed that their laughter broke the tension and everyone returned to normal and experienced a very productive annual meeting.

Stories do more than clarify a bigger picture. Stories and analogies have a way of moving people more quickly through those valleys and moments of despair that we all experience in life. Even a story of failure and not achieving results becomes a providential story when made useful with follow-up questions like: If you had the power to change your story what would you change? What would you do differently? And how can you apply this to our current crisis? How can this story help us figure out a path looking backward from our desired state?

I have heard it said that "Facts tell, and stories sell." The visionary leader in any organization (be it sales, manufacturing, retail, finance, or health care) models this for his or her people and for the collective success of his or her organization.

Wright

If the visionary is categorized as a management competency or one set of leadership behaviors, does any special correlation of visionary role model practices exist with other management competencies?

Zimmerman

I think that the visionary or strategic practice is the leadership currency for success, that's how I'll phrase it. Thinking of money as valuable currency, the visionary practices become useful leaders' currency for realizing other management practices (and gains). Visionary practice invigorates how leaders coach, communicate, build relationships among diverse people, how they resolve conflict, and how they motivate teams that can produce without constant direction. And the visionary behaviors become a gateway enabling other successful leadership behaviors. Visionary leaders ask questions that prompt people to think in new ways and ask questions like, "What is it you most want to have happen?" A question like this enables effective coaching and developing of people because they enable people to respond from more than just their head.

Another example is when leaders develop an orientation of team. I regularly heard visionary role model leaders comment to me that they were not natural storytellers, but that they recognized there were natural ones in every group. When the group was stuck on a particular issue or circumstance, the leader would ask, "Does this remind anybody of a situation you have previously been in?" Eventually someone in the group would relate a story and the effect on the group was that it helped them to get un-stuck. It's as if hearing the story freed people from this temporary mindset of paralysis. This demonstrates a leader's ability to foster a team orientation—a team thinking together. So it's not that the leaders necessarily are the ones who have to always ask the same questions differently or share the story. They encourage their employees to ask the same question differently and to develop a local culture of storytelling.

There may be a stronger correlation to being decisive and taking risks. Not being a whiner, not thinking "shoulda, coulda, woulda," but rather learning from decisions, constructively challenging the status quo, and always trying new ideas or approaches.

Wright

Will you further describe this correlation to being decisive and taking risks?

Zimmerman

Some role model visionaries suggested to me that the risk-taking and decisive behaviors of leadership are sisters to visionary and strategic thinking. That's how they referred to it. In their view the visionary's propensity to open possibilities and ask questions in a different way and to get people to think rather than just follow procedures makes decisiveness and risk-taking a natural follow-through. It's this creation of decisions and opportunities for taking risks that is a byproduct of the practice of visionary behaviors. It's that eternal flame that flickers bright on our future. It's a flicker of clarity that enables people to both honor the past and continually create the future. This sounds a little philosophical, but there is a deeper practice and results to back this up.

For example, James Burke, the CEO back in the days of the Tylenol-cyanide poisonings, asked a lot of questions of different people and he developed a solution. He recommended his solution to the Board of Directors of Johnson & Johnson. The proposed solution was to take all Tylenol off the shelves worldwide, destroy them, and then re-package the newly manufactured Tylenol in tamper-proof containers and redistribute them.

I heard that the directors initially replied, "No, this is too expensive an option."

"Not doing it will not only cost you your CEO, but your good name and reputation," Burke countered.

The Board re-voted and endorsed his recommendation. James Burke's vision and practice of visionary behaviors led to his recommendation and conviction. He was willing to take the risk of unemployment. Would you agree that now we benefit from the added security that tamper-proof packaging of over-the-counter drugs offer to this day? Would we call this a success?

Wright

Any other special correlation of the visionary leadership style to other management competencies?

Zimmerman

As a frame supports its structure, visionary behaviors support leadership practice. Visionary behaviors become a gateway to other leadership competencies that I mentioned before, such as: resolving conflict, integrity, developing relationships, and meeting clients' needs as the situation requires. It makes leadership more than a success by chance. Visionary practices create successful leadership even in the worst of times.

If you don't mind, I'd like to ask you a question, David.

Wright

Go right ahead.

Zimmerman

I know this firsthand about you—I know that you live out your purpose and you've done this with a vision yourself. As a successful business entrepreneur, how do you personally relate to our discussion today, based on your personal experience? What would *you* add? In other words, does this remind you of some of your own personal practices? And is there anything else that comes to mind for you that would demonstrate visionary behaviors?

Wright

Of course—I'm in agreement with almost if not all of the things you have said. When I look back on the times I've been really successful and when I have shown some of these characteristics of a visionary person, one of the things I have a lot of problems with is the ability to explain it through stories or examples.

I have a workshop coming up for professional speakers and professional authors. One of the things I don't think they're getting is that things can't change 180 degrees as easily as you can incrementally *add* to it. I've got a lot of things I'm going to do on a PowerPoint presentation. I'm going to trace Dagwood and Blondie all the way back to 1933, and I'm going to show them every ten years up until today to illustrate how they have not changed. I'm going to demonstrate that concept with many other examples. I'm going to show the development of the Morton Salt girl, you know, "*When it rains, it pours*"? And I'm going to show that nothing has changed since 1939 except the dress styles and her hair styles.

People understand concepts when they have something to hang on to, that's why the study of history is so helpful. That's why we like to walk through museums and that's why people my age like to look back. When a young man comes into my office and asks me to "change," what he's asking me to do is get rid of sixty-seven years of wisdom, if he wants me to change a hundred and eighty degrees!

So, yes, I think that everything you've said here is right on.

Zimmerman

When I think about what you said—the notion of the one eighty—to me a change like that might occur because of a significant emotional experience. The death of someone who was trying to share something with me that I wasn't listening to, and the moment that person passes away it finally just hits me and I immediately make a one eighty.

But you're right. You remind me of a leadership philosopher named Peter Koestenbaum. He would coach CEOs on leadership, and one of the things that fascinated me about him, and that I learned from him, is that human history back through ancient times, as we study all the major events that occurred, reflect the individual decisions of people and their individual thinking. Collectively they then become those stories of history. This reminds me that we continue to create our history. We do so based upon our own individual thinking, and thinking with others around us.

I look forward to seeing how that goes with your workshop and how people will receive that; your idea sounds neat.

Wright

What do you consider the most important bottom-line benefit of practicing visionary behaviors at work?

Zimmerman

I'd say simplifying the big picture so that people can decide, they can take risks, and they can effectively focus on their contribution to the whole. For example, there's Admiral "Bull" Halsey in World War II. Of course, being the U.S. Naval Academy graduate that he was, I like to quote him. He stated, "Hit 'em hard, hit 'em fast, hit 'em often." This was not a wordy command full of details or "how to's," but this suggested to his organization of sailors what to do within the context of their specific and varied jobs. To the gunners in ordnance it translated into keeping their guns at the ready and their ammo in supply; it suggested to the signal men to be prepared for around-the-clock emergency communication to other ships on a moment's notice in all conditions; to the cooks it meant preparing for meals at times other than just normal meal times, and preparing for interruptions to those meals. That one phrase, "hit 'em hard, hit 'em fast, hit 'em often," suggested to people in different jobs in different parts of the organization what they needed to do. It communicated attitude. It also presupposed and trusted that people knew their jobs.

The bottom-line benefit is people in organizational performance adapt in changing times and especially in adversity. "Hit 'em hard, hit 'em fast, hit 'em often" visionary leaders teach people to think as a leader, not what to think, which is leader-led. Maybe I should repeat that, because I think it's so important: visionary leaders teach people to think like a leader—not what to think.

Wright

Like you, I probably believe one of the greatest learning models is the answering of questions. Sometimes I like to ask myself questions that have always been hard for me to answer. When you consider our readers, the people who are now reading this chapter, do you have some questions you would like to leave with them for consideration?

Zimmerman

Sure, and I'll have to say that this is not the complete list, but these are some starter questions readers can think about that may speak to them in particular situations.

First: Formulate *leader-full* questions. Ask yourself if the answer suggests an immediate reply or does it require living with the question for answers to emerge from within, whether it's from within the group or from within the individual over time? In other words, am I really asking a question that just requires me to find information right there out of a book or a Web site, or is it the kind of a question that requires me to think and to grow?

Second: Do I really believe that asking better questions results in better answers?

Third: How can this be just as important across varying environments? Is the practice of visionary behaviors equally effective across varying environments such as the manufacturing plant floor, the doctor's office, the retail showroom, the bank or credit union lobby, the school classroom, the locker room, a court of law, the military briefing session, the halls of legislature, and the executive boardroom?

Fourth: How do these practices support the experience that "less can be more?"

Fifth: If I had the power to change the story, what would I change? How would I change it? How is this about facilitating change as the norm, not change as the exception—not change as the enemy forced on us?

Sixth: Recall a time when I stumbled on an idea and followed it through. What thoughts most precipitated my idea? What question or questions do I recall asking prior to my idea taking form? Do I routinely share these kinds of questions with others around me or do I keep these questions to myself internal in my own mind?

Seventh: Am I known for asking the questions that prompt people to see and think differently?

Eighth: How is this about promoting success? How does the habit of a visionary promote surrounding myself with successful and thinking people?

Ninth: What habits just described remind me of me, or remind me of someone I know?

Tenth: Who could I seek as a mentor to help me develop my visionary and strategic thinking habits, which will contribute to my future success?

Finally: What motivates me more—maximizing shareholder value or a compelling story or a vision of a future I helped to create through my talents, skills, and attentiveness wrapped in commitment?

I'll conclude with a story.

An interviewer had asked Mother Teresa many years ago, "What makes you think you can eradicate the plight of the poor around the world when whole countries and organizations have tried and failed?"

She responded, "I am not called to be successful; I am called to be faithful."

Considering Mother Teresa's comment to what am I called, what changes for me when I think in terms of being faithful, not just in terms of being successful?

Did the reader notice the caption at the foot of the front cover about sharpening your pencil? Having been introduced as the greatest woman in the world, Mother Teresa walked up to the speaker's stand and began, "If you think I was the greatest, you think God would have made me a little taller. I am not the greatest woman, but I'll tell you who I am. I am a tiny pencil in the mighty hand of God, through whom God writes love letters to the world."

My hope is that our book sharpens your tiny pencil. What letter is your life writing to the world?

I welcome readers to send me stories, experiences, and questions. And I really thank you, David, for the opportunity to share some of this in this book.

Wright

These are great questions, and I've written them down and I'm going to think about them over the weekend.

Today we've been talking with Marty Zimmerman. Thank you so much, Marty, for being here with us on *Speaking of Success*.

About the Author

Born and raised in Cincinnati, Marty Zimmerman attended a seminary after high school to become a priest. Changing his career path, he received an appointment to the Naval Academy, Annapolis, Maryland. Upon graduation, he entered the Marine Corps, retiring after twenty-two years (active and reserve).

He served in corporate management/executive leadership development for a Fortune 100 company for nine years. His extensive global experience as a leadership and executive performance coach became the source of his insightful stories as a speaker, author, and coach. His learning became the source for his first published book, *In Their Presence: Best Practices and Stories of Role Models*.

He speaks to the best practices of role model leaders and facilitates half-day and full-day organizational leadership development seminars. As a leadership consultant, he offers leadership and executive performance coaching and feedback. He is a member of the International Speakers Network.

Married with two daughters, he has lived in Michigan since 1987. He enjoys jogging, swimming, and eating ice cream.

Marty Zimmerman
In Their Presence Leadership
7071 Snow Apple Drive
Clarkston, MI 48346
Phone: 248.895.0016
E-mail: marty@intheirpresence.com
www.intheirpresence.com

Chapter 6

Rose Mary Hefley

THE INTERVIEW

David Wright (Wright)

Today we are talking with Rose Mary Hefley. After more than twenty years in the corporate business world/she began her own consulting firm, Achievement Unlimited, Inc., in 1994. Since that time she has helped hundreds of organizations increase profitability and productivity. Her coaching and training reputation is built on what works and what doesn't. She draws on personal stories from her years of experiences as an entrepreneur, business executive, sales manager, and plant supervisor.

Before creating Achievement Unlimited, Rose Mary held leadership positions for Mutual of Omaha, Browning-Ferris Industries, Meredith Publishing Co., Montgomery Ward, and Stanley Home Products.

Rose Mary, welcome to *Speaking of Success*!

Rose Mary Hefley (Hefley)

Thank you so much!

Wright

Business seems to get harder each year. How can business owners set themselves apart to achieve their goals despite a tough and competitive business environment?

Hefley

Ask yourself this question: *what are you going to do to make this year your best year yet?*

How will you measure success this year compared with last year? It's a trick question. Many people measure success in terms of the car they drive, the bonuses, award plaques on the wall, the number of clients, business trips, direct reports, and thickness of the carpet in their office.

Perhaps the most important measures of success are internal rather than external. No matter how much we accumulate and accomplish, we have to stand in front of the mirror and feel good about the person looking back.

The difference between highly successful and happy people is the way they think about life. Perhaps the most important measures of success, then, are the internal victories rather than the external.

Success can be measured in many ways. No doubt, the measure of success is in the attitude we have developed over the years. Habit of thought is the way I define attitude. What is your view of the world? Is it one of abundance and opportunity or do you see a place of scarcity and hopelessness?

The way we view the world depends much on the conditioning we have received from other well-meaning and influential people in our lives starting with our parents and moving through life to our work contacts, the bosses we have encountered, and our colleagues. Everyone we meet helps shape our world view.

Our world view may work well for us or it may not. What is important is that you and I know what actions we take that cause us to achieve the results that we want, and we know how to correct what works against us or does not work for us. For us to change our results in any area, we must first make the decision to take action to bring about that change. In other words, "change our conditions by changing our attitude of mind."

"The most important single discovery of this generation
is that we change our conditions by
changing our attitude of mind."—William James

Wright

Do you agree that strong and appropriate leadership is the key to success in corporate America today?

Hefley

I believe that good leadership is the key to success in any business. My clients often ask me why they don't accomplish their goals. The answers are quite simple; they must learn to make success a habit—not a goal. I break it down into five simple rules.

In business we have learned there are basically five reasons why employers and employees don't accomplish what they need to. Here's how to make success a habit for yourself in your business endeavors and for your company:

1. **Employees must know what to do.** Most people want to do a good job. Ah, but if they only understood what a good job looks like. What one person may consider a good job may not fit the specifications of another.

Leaders must make the vision, purpose, and values of the organization clear. It's important to provide job descriptions that clearly identify expectations that determine success in a particular position. Leaders provide feedback and evaluations so that employees know when they're doing a good job (and when they aren't).

Communicate what success is. Reinforce it. Success becomes a habit. Good leaders may know this intuitively or may have learned it along the way.

Yes, leadership skills can be learned. I don't think anybody is a born leader. I think that people are born with certain characteristics, and as they develop they can improve upon those characteristics. But leadership is not something you learn overnight. I believe it's a process.

There are leadership techniques you can learn, and if you learn them gradually and implement them as you're learning them—and tracking and measuring your performance—you're going to be able to have something solid and something lasting.

A leader, therefore, is a visionary. Being the visionary and then communicating that vision to the right people, putting them in the right positions, teaching them the skills and the knowledge that they need to perform their functions—that's leadership. Then get out of their way.

2. Employees must know how to do a good job. Let me share a story about a young woman who was supervising in a light manufacturing plant. The plant was a start-up operation, and this rooky was responsible for getting the plant operational and for insuring the success of the operation once it started running. A daunting task? Yes.

The plant opened on time and the operations started to smooth out. It was very important to this young supervisor for everyone in the plant to perform up to maximum capability. This meant that employees needed to be on time, to do their job correctly, and to perform in a manner that was professional and safe.

The biggest problem was that many of the workers didn't have a sense of urgency when it came to accomplishing tasks. When work needed to be done, people needed to be in the right place at the right time doing the right things. There was no time for chit-chat. The supervisor had work to do and expectations to meet. Those who didn't comply were fired.

About nine months after plant opening, our young heroine's plant was visited by the VP of Operations. The VP expressed gratitude to the supervisor for her commitment to the project. He went on to say that, even though they appreciated her effort and hard work, perhaps they had made a mistake in hiring her.

What? She was shocked. As it turned out, her plant had the highest turnover rate of all their plants in the country. The VP informed her that when the turnover is as high as it was in her plant, it is not the fault of the employees, but lack of leadership and management skills—on *her part.* Even though our heroine had the background and the technical skills for the position, she lacked the empathy and knowledge to lead people.

Our young supervisor, of course, was stunned to think that other people were criticizing her performance when they just didn't understand how hard her job was. She believed that workers who did not want to cooperate had to be let go, and if they didn't want to work under the conditions that required them to do their job *right,* they could leave. Her life lesson was about to begin.

The VP presented her with three options: She could resign. Together they would develop a cover story to protect her and the organization. Or, two, she could be fired. Again, they would agree on a cover story to protect her reputation and the organization's. Or, three, she could agree to learn what she didn't know about what she didn't know and be on a six-month probation.

Our heroine moved quickly from being "unconsciously incompetent" to becoming aware that she was "consciously incompetent." She had a choice to make. She could blame others, react from fear, and be angry, or she could choose the path of integrity and make choices that allowed her to improve and redeem herself. She chose to learn what she didn't know about what she didn't know.

Today she is grateful that her employer gave her an opportunity to grow as a leader and as an individual. So my challenge to you is this: Ask yourself what you could do better. The signs are all there. Are you aware of the direction they are pointing you?

Many people are over-managed but under-led. When employees are empowered and clear about their objectives, and if they have the ability to execute, they can't help but be successful. In fact, I think that instead of referring to the people in the organization as *employees*, if you really work with providing them the information that they need, they can become *partners* in the success of that organization.

I conduct sales training for various organizations and always find it interesting that as we are talking about organizational development and companies are hiring people, they say, "We only hire experienced salespeople because if they have sold before, they'll be successful for us." And then something happens and we find out they're *not* successful. Why?

It is important to provide new hires with training about your organization and about what makes your organization special. If you don't provide employees with the opportunity to learn the skills that you want them to know in your organization, you are short-changing that employee and you are short-changing yourself.

Training is not a luxury. It's a necessity. You are helping employees become successful. *The only thing worse than losing a trained employee is keeping an untrained one.* With that said, the question that comes to mind is this: what do you need to learn how to do to be more successful and to make this your best year yet?

Many times when I begin a new supervisory and leadership program, there is some resistance from the participants. At the beginning of the class the most often-asked question is this one: how do I get employees to do what I want them to do? At about the midway point in the class, the light bulb goes on. These same people finally realize they didn't know what they didn't know. Think about it.

3. People may not be as effective as they could be because they are not in an environment that supports their success or perhaps they don't have the necessary resources. They have two choices: communicate what they need (and why) to someone who can do something about it, or leave the environment.

You've heard this before, but it bears repeating here: people don't leave companies, they leave bosses. At least 21 percent of all turnover happens because employees do not like their environment (read that: bosses). Again, choices can be made.

When we have done surveys of employees to find out what type of training they felt was necessary, the overwhelming majority of those responding felt that communication was a real issue in their workplaces. Lack of communication! What you might find interesting is that communication is about the least taught skill. If you do not have effective communication from the top of your organization, the people who are expected to do the work will not be able to perform in a satisfactory manner.

So what needs to be communicated? The vision of the organization, the purpose, and the values, the code of conduct, if you will. If the leaders of the organization are not clear about their vision, mission, purpose, and core values, then the rest of the company is not going to be able to meet expectations. Every employee deserves to know where he or she fits in an organization. Employees deserve job descriptions and feedback on performance. They deserve to be coached and mentored and treated the way they want to be treated.

A leader must communicate effectively. A leader must also provide the training and development and to make sure that employees have a safe environment and that employees have all the resources they need to do the job. For example, are there enough people in a department to accomplish the tasks? Are the computers loaded with the right software to do the work?

Environment, of course, doesn't mean the temperature is too hot or too cold! I'm talking about stress and tension levels. Low morale and lowered productivity. Twenty-one percent of turnover comes from people who don't want to be working in a particular environment anymore. Almost a fourth of a workforce at any one time may not be happy with the environment—the boss. They will be leaving you.

I think that much of the stress in today's workplace comes from employees not wanting to be where they are—at work. They're not bad people, they just weren't trained properly. They don't have the resources to do their jobs, because no one communicated the company goals and expectations. A flawed hiring process coupled with poor or no training is now showing up as low morale and high level of tension and stress. Sound familiar?

In a recent non-managerial survey, only 25 percent of employees responded they felt engaged and took pride in their work. Another 25 percent felt they could be more productive, and the rest (50 percent) said they were only putting enough time and effort and energy into their jobs to keep their jobs. For a business owner this is scary. That means there is a lot of waste in the organization.

Stress happens when people don't know where they're going or what they're doing or why they're doing it. Some stress is good stress—even productive and creative. But the *bad* stress occurs when employees are constantly putting out fires. People don't come to work for *our* reasons; they come to work for *their* reasons.

When employees are given the opportunity to set their own goals, when they understand where they fit in the organization, when they understand the importance of the role they play on a team, they will generate good stress versus bad stress. I believe that when people know who they are, where they are going, and how to get there, then the stress is not a big factor.

4. Employees may not be successful because they just don't have the aptitude. There are a lot of things I can't do. I could not take a car or a computer apart and put it back together. Guess what? I don't want to either. I also know I don't have the aptitude to be in a stationary position for a long period of time. My energy level is too high. I need to move around. I am good at speaking, listening, and problem-solving, but not administrative or routine tasks. So if you're trying to put a round peg into a square hole, it isn't going to fit.

I recommend that, when companies are hiring people who are the "right fit" for the organization, communicate your vision and passion for your business. Look for people who resonate with that same energy. More than 66 percent of all hires prove to be mistakes within the first year.

My fellow Omahan, Warren Buffett, has often been quoted as saying, "If you are looking for someone to hire, you want them to have integrity, intelligence, and energy. If they don't have the first, you really want to hire them dumb and lazy because the other two will kill you." The leadership of any organization must be quite clear about the direction they want to go and be very effective about communicating that direction to the right people.

The lesson here: hire the right people doing the right things in the right order, and you will increase their chances (and yours) to be successful.

5. **Employees need to want to be successful.** How many people do you know who say that they should quit smoking, but continue to smoke? Until they decide they want to quit, they won't. There are payoffs to hanging onto vices, and there are payoffs to staying stuck.

Wright

Those are great rules to follow for any size business. Your philosophy really demonstrates that success is a habit. Do you believe that any person can change his or her mindset and put these rules into action?

Hefley

Quite frankly, you may find that employees don't do what you want them to do because they just don't want to. That's what we would call an "attitude," and if it's an attitude problem, then we need to find out what went wrong. And chances are the problem can be pinpointed to one of these areas: communication, training, or environment. In that case you will need to find a way either to correct that, or to make the tough decision and let the person go. It's the job of the leader to make the people on your team successful.

"We cannot become what we need to be
by remaining what we are."—Max DePree

Wright

You talk about organizations setting themselves apart from the competition. What steps can a business take now and how can they plan for competitive threats in the future?

Hefley

I ask my clients, "Can you clearly identify and communicate what makes you different?"

What differentiates your organization from your competitors? Is your quality consistent time after time after time? Is it the fact that you are faster than somebody else at producing an item? Is it the fact that you have employees who are going to make the difference?

To give you an example, I differentiate my consulting services by finding out in advance what results our clients are expecting. Then we design our programs to meet their expectations. We meet with each individual and set measurable objectives so we can have win/win outcomes. I don't consider it "training" to put on a workshop without interaction and follow-up. I consider that *information delivery*. Training without behavior change is entertainment. If our clients can't measure results, we don't know whether what we do is working or not.

What added value can you give your clients?

"Added value" can be something as simple as a beauty salon adding a scalp massage that takes an extra minute or two without charging for it. Or my salon provides a free hand wax when you purchase two services. This might be a simple example, but it's just one of those simple things that doesn't cost a lot, but the customers remember how the experience made them feel when they were there. That's value added.

As I look at my business—the business of developing people—I see a value added service in this way: After we have worked with an organization, we call back and check to see how people are doing. We want to know what worked for them. We may do some extra training just to keep the momentum going.

Wright

Let's talk about "value added" for a minute. Can you give our readers an example of value added services that increased profits by implementing an added value to a company's clients?

Hefley

Any business can find some value added service. That's what will set your business apart from the competitors in this global economy.

In order for any business to be more successful, each individual must be more successful. My program, called *Great Habits for Success: A Plan for Living,* teaches the basic principles so each of us can conquer life. We guide people in making choices to win the inner victory.

To do so, however, you must learn to value and respect yourself at a very deep level so that in turn you will value and respect other people. You make choices based on your purpose and mission. In other words, we all make choices, take responsibility for our outcomes, and lead with integrity. I call it "getting out of your own way."

When we understand the paradigms from which we live our lives, we'll be able to change the paradigms that don't work for ones that do work because life is about choices. Daily we are faced with changes, challenges, and choices. A successful leader decides on success. If you want to be a successful leader, you will learn to take action to live your life by practicing personal and business leadership habits. Success depends on your ability to take personal responsibility for the choices you make at work and in your personal relationships.

When I ask people to make a list of their strengths and to make a list of their limitations, the list of limitations is usually longer than their list of strengths. Why? Because people are continually trying to fix themselves. And they will find that life is going to be hard for them.

But when people start living from their strengths, when they recognize their strengths and start building on them through success habits, then the limitations are not nearly as, well, limiting. We are all flawed human beings. But when we can accept ourselves for who we are, and when we can move beyond that, we will be able to accept others and see the strengths in them and not just their limitations.

Wright

If I were to open a new business today, what advice would you give me to ensure that I am successful?

Hefley

Let me answer that by asking this question: so what is success to you? Is it winning the battle of negativity within yourself or your company, is it losing weight, is it finally making peace with someone with whom you've been estranged, is it finding your dream job, is it starting your own business, is it finally hiring the right team to grow your business? Is success taking your department or your company to its next level? Is it finishing your degree? What is it that is holding you back from being excited by life?

As we sum up what affects our businesses and our environments, success really has to do with relationships. Our attitude affects the quality of our relationships—and that's the heart of customer services.

It's about relationships, isn't it? So which factors affecting our relationships do we need to handle better? It could be the way we handle our emotions, our time commitments, our self-image, our health, education, finances, and self-esteem. All of these things affect our opinion of ourselves.

I challenge you to set goals to make this your best year yet. What areas do you need to set goals in? What changes do you need to make? When are you going to make them? This could be your best year yet. Are you ready, willing, and able?

I am an admirer of nature. My favorite bird is the eagle. It is glorious, powerful, and never misses its target. The eagle is my logo because it represents precision. I believe there is an eagle in all of us just waiting to be pushed out of the nest.

So, set your goals high. Believe that when you do the right things for the right reasons, in the right order, that you will accomplish anything you set out to do with the precision of the eagle. You can do it!

Success is a choice. Success is a habit.

About the Author

Rose Mary Hefley is President of Achievement Unlimited, Inc. Her Omaha-based firm teaches personal and organizational leadership nationally. Prior to founding Achievement Unlimited, Inc., she served in leadership roles at Meredith Publishing, Browning-Ferris Industries, and Mutual of Omaha. She is a sought-after speaker and coach on leadership, revenue generation, and personal effectiveness.

Rose Mary Hefley
Achievement Unlimited, Inc.
8732 Polk St.
Omaha, NE 68127
Phone: 402.597.1447
E-mail: rosemary@successisahabit.com
www.SuccessIsAHabit.com

Chapter 7

JACK CANFIELD

THE INTERVIEW

David E. Wright (Wright)

Today we are talking with Jack Canfield. You probably know him as the founder and co-creator of the *New York Times* number one best-selling *Chicken Soup for the Soul* book series. As of 2006 there are sixty-five titles and eighty million copies in print in over thirty-seven languages.

Jack's background includes a BA from Harvard, a master's from the University of Massachusetts, and an Honorary Doctorate from the University of Santa Monica. He has been a high school and university teacher, a workshop facilitator, a psychotherapist, and a leading authority in the area of self-esteem and personal development.

Jack Canfield, welcome to *Speaking of Success.*

Jack Canfield (Canfield)

Thank you, David. It's great to be with you.

Wright

I talked with Mark Victor Hansen a few days ago. He gave you full credit for coming up with the idea of the *Chicken Soup* series. Obviously it's made you an internationally known personality. Other than recognition, has the series changed you personally and if so, how?

Canfield

I would say that it has and I think in a couple of ways. Number one, I read stories all day long of people who've overcome what would feel like insurmountable obstacles. For example, we just did a book *Chicken Soup for the Unsinkable Soul.* There's a story in there about a single mother with three daughters. She contracted a disease and she had to have both of her hands and both of her feet amputated. She got prosthetic devices and was able to learn how to use them. She could cook, drive the car, brush her daughters' hair, get a job, etc. I read that and I thought, "God, what would I ever have to complain and whine and moan about?"

At one level it's just given me a great sense of gratitude and appreciation for everything I have and it has made me less irritable about the little things.

I think the other thing that's happened for me personally is my sphere of influence has changed. By that I mean I was asked, for example, a couple of years ago to be the keynote speaker to the Women's Congressional Caucus. The Caucus is a group that includes all women in America who are members of Congress and who are state senators, governors, and lieutenant governors. I asked what they wanted me to talk about—what topic.

"Whatever you think we need to know to be better legislators," was the reply.

I thought, "Wow, they want me to tell them about what laws they should be making and what would make a better culture." Well, that wouldn't have happened if our books hadn't come out and I hadn't become famous. I think I get to play with people at a higher level and have more influence in the world. That's important to me because my life purpose is inspiring and empowering people to live their highest vision so the world works for everybody. I get to do that on a much bigger level than when I was just a high school teacher back in Chicago.

Wright

I think one of the powerful components of that book series is that you can read a positive story in just a few minutes and come back and revisit it. I know my daughter has three of the books and she just reads them interchangeably. Sometimes I go in her bedroom and she'll be crying and reading one of them. Other times she'll be laughing, so they really are "chicken soup for the soul," aren't they?

Canfield

They really are. In fact we have four books in the *Teenage Soul* series now and a new one coming out at the end of this year. I have a son who's eleven and he has a twelve-year-old friend who's a girl. We have a new book called *Chicken Soup for the Teenage Soul and the Tough Stuff.* It's all about dealing with parents' divorces, teachers who don't understand you, boyfriends who drink and drive, and other issues pertinent to that age group. I asked my son's friend, "Why do you like this book?" (It's our most popular book among teens right now.) She said, "You know, whenever I'm feeling down I read it and it makes me cry and I feel better. Some of the stories make me laugh and some of the stories make me feel more responsible for my life. But basically I just feel like I'm not alone."

One of the people I work with recently said that the books are like a support group between the covers of a book—you can read about other peoples' experiences and realize you're not the only one going through something.

Wright

Jack, with our *Speaking of Success* series we're trying to encourage people in our audience to be better, to live better, and be more fulfilled by reading about the experiences of our writers. Is there anyone or anything in your life that has made a difference for you and helped you to become a better person?

Canfield

Yes and we could do ten books just on that. I'm influenced by people all the time. If I were to go way back I'd have to say one of the key influences in my life was Jesse Jackson when he was still a minister in Chicago. I was teaching in an all black high school there and I went to Jesse Jackson's church with a friend one time. What happened for me was that I saw somebody with a vision. (This was before Martin Luther King was killed and Jesse was of the lieutenants in his organization.) I just saw people trying to make the world work better for a certain segment of the population. I was inspired by that kind of visionary belief that it's possible to make change.

Later on, John F. Kennedy was a hero of mine. I was very much inspired by him.

Another is a therapist by the name of Robert Resnick. He was my therapist for two years. He taught me a little formula called E + R = O that stands for Events + Response = Outcome. He said, "If you don't like your outcomes quit blaming the events and start changing your responses." One of his favorite phrases was, "If the grass on the other side of the fence looks greener, start watering your own lawn more."

I think he helped me get off any kind of self-pity I might have had because I had parents who were alcoholics. It would have been very easy to blame them for problems I might have had. They weren't very successful or rich; I was surrounded by people who were and I felt like, "God, what if I'd had parents like they had? I could have been a lot better." He just got me off that whole notion and made me realize the hand you were dealt is the hand you've got to play and take responsibility for who you are and quit complaining and blaming others and get on with your life. That was a turning point for me.

I'd say the last person who really affected me big time was a guy named W. Clement Stone who was a self-made multi-millionaire in Chicago. He taught me that success is not a four-letter word—it's nothing to be ashamed of—and you ought to go for it. He said, "The best thing you can do for the poor is not be one of them." Be a model for what it is to live a successful life. So I learned from him the principles of success and that's what I've been teaching now for more than thirty years.

Wright

He was an entrepreneur in the insurance industry, wasn't he?

Canfield

He was. He had combined insurance. When I worked for him he was worth 600 million dollars and that was before the dot.com millionaires came along in Silicon Valley. He just knew more about success. He was a good friend of Napoleon Hill (author of *Think and Grow Rich)* and he was a fabulous mentor. I really learned a lot from him.

Wright

I miss some of the men I listened to when I was a young salesman coming up and he was one of them. Napoleon Hill was another one as was Dr. Peale. All of their writings made me who I am today. I'm glad I had that opportunity.

Canfield

One speaker whose name you probably will remember, Charlie "Tremendous" Jones, says, "Who we are is a result of the books we read and the people we hang out with." I think that's so true and that's why I tell people, "If you want to have high self-esteem, hang out with people who have high self-esteem. If you want to be more spiritual, hang out with spiritual people." We're always telling our children, "Don't hang out with those kids." The reason we don't want them to is because we know how influential people are with each other. I think we need to give ourselves the same advice. Who are we hanging out with? We can hang out with them in books, cassette tapes, CDs, radio shows, and in person.

Wright

One of my favorites was a fellow named Bill Gove from Florida. I talked with him about three or four years ago. He's retired now. His mind is still as quick as it ever was. I thought he was one of the greatest speakers I had ever heard.

What do you think makes up a great mentor? In other words, are there characteristics that mentors seem to have in common?

Canfield

I think there are two obvious ones. I think mentors have to have the time to do it and the willingness to do it. I also think they need to be people who are doing something you want to do. W. Clement Stone used to tell me, "If you want to be rich, hang out with rich people. Watch what they do, eat what they eat, dress the way they dress. Try it on." He wasn't suggesting that you give up your authentic self, but he was pointing out that rich people probably have habits that you don't have and you should study them.

I always ask salespeople in an organization, "Who are the top two or three in your organization?" I tell them to start taking them out to lunch and dinner and for a drink and finding out what they do. Ask them, "What's your secret?" Nine times out of ten they'll be willing to tell you.

This goes back to what we said earlier about asking. I'll go into corporations and I'll say, "Who are the top ten people?" They'll all tell me and I'll say, "Did you ever ask them what they do different than you?"

"No," they'll reply.

"Why not?"

"Well, they might not want to tell me."

"How do you know? Did you ever ask them? All they can do is say no. You'll be no worse off than you are now."

So I think with mentors you just look at people who seem to be living the life you want to live and achieving the results you want to achieve.

What we say in our book is when that you approach a mentor they're probably busy and successful and so they haven't got a lot of time. Just ask, "Can I talk to you for ten minutes every month?" If I know it's only going to be ten minutes I'll probably say yes. The neat thing is if I like you I'll always give you more than ten minutes, but that ten minutes gets you in the door.

Wright

In the future are there any more Jack Canfield books authored singularly?

Canfield

One of my books includes the formula I mentioned earlier: E + R = O. I just felt I wanted to get that out there because every time I give a speech and I talk about that the whole room gets so quiet that you could hear a pin drop—I can tell people are really getting value. Then I'm going to do a series of books on the principles of success. I've got about 150 of them that I've identified over the years. I have a book down the road I want to do that's called *No More Put-Downs,* which is a book probably aimed mostly at parents, teacher and managers. There's a culture we have now of put-down humor. Whether it's *Married With Children* or *All in the Family,* there's that characteristic of macho put-down humor. There's research now showing how bad it is for kids' self-esteem when the coaches do it so I want to get that message out there as well.

Wright

It's really not that funny, is it?

Canfield

No, we'll laugh it off because we don't want to look like we're a wimp but underneath we're hurt. The research now shows that you're better off breaking a child's bones than you are breaking their spirit. A bone will heal much more quickly than their emotional spirit will.

Wright

I remember recently reading a survey where people listed the top five people who had influenced them. I've tried it on a couple of groups at church and in other places. In my case, and in the survey, approximately three out of the top five are always teachers. I wonder if that's going to be the same in the next decade.

Canfield

I think that's probably because as children we're at our most formative years. We actually spend more time with our teachers than we do with our parents. Research shows that the average parent only interacts verbally with each of their children only about eight and a half minutes a day. Yet at school they're interacting with their teachers for anywhere from six to eight hours depending on how long the school day is, including coaches, chorus directors, etc.

I think that in almost everybody's life there's been that one teacher who loved him or her as a human being—an individual—not just one of the many students the teacher was supposed to fill full of History and English. That teacher believed in you and inspired you.

Les Brown is one of the great motivational speakers in the world. If it hadn't been for one teacher who said, "I think you can do more than be in a special ed. class. I think you're the one," he'd probably still be cutting grass in the median strip of the highways in Florida instead of being a $35,000-a-talk speaker.

Wright

I had a conversation one time with Les. He told me about this wonderful teacher who discovered Les was dyslexic. Everybody else called him dumb and this one lady just took him under her wing and had him tested. His entire life changed because of her interest in him.

Canfield

I'm on the board of advisors of the Dyslexic Awareness Resource Center here in Santa Barbara. The reason is because I taught high school with a lot of kids who were called at-risk—kids who would end up in gangs and so forth. What we found over and over was that about 78 percent of all the kids in the juvenile detention centers in Chicago were kids who had learning disabilities—primarily dyslexia—but there were others as well. They were never diagnosed and they weren't doing well in school so they'd drop out. As soon as a student drops out of school he or she becomes subject to the influence of gangs and other kinds of criminal and drug linked activities. If these kids had been diagnosed earlier we'd get rid of a large amount of the juvenile crime in America because there are a lot of really good programs that can teach dyslexics to read and excel in school.

Wright

My wife is a teacher and she brings home stories that are heartbreaking about parents not being as concerned with their children as they used to be, or at least not as helpful as they used to be. Did you find that to be a problem when you were teaching?

Canfield

It depends on what kind of district you're in. If it's a poor district the parents could be on drugs, alcoholics, and basically just not available. If you're in a really high rent district the parents not available because they're both working, coming home tired, they're jet-setters, or they're working late at the office because they're workaholics. Sometimes it just legitimately takes two paychecks to pay the rent anymore.

I find that the majority of parents care but often they don't know what to do. They don't know how to discipline their children. They don't know how to help them with their homework. They can't pass on skills that they never acquired themselves. Unfortunately, the trend tends to be like a chain letter. The people with the least amount of skills tend to have the most number of children. The other thing is that you get crack babies (infants born addicted to crack cocaine because of the mother's addiction). In Los Angeles one out of every ten babies born is a crack baby.

Wright

That's unbelievable.

Canfield

Yes and another statistic is that by the time 50 percent of the kids are twelve years old they have started experimenting with alcohol. I see a lot of that in the Bible belt. The problem is not the big city, urban designer drugs but alcoholism. Another thing you get, unfortunately, is a lot of let's call it familial violence—kids getting beat up, parents who drink and then explode—child abuse and sexual abuse. You see a lot of that.

Wright

Most people are fascinated by these television shows about being a survivor. What has been the greatest comeback that you have made from adversity in your career or in your life?

Canfield

You know it's funny, I don't think I've had a lot of major failures and setbacks where I had to start over. My life's been on an intentional curve. But I do have a lot of challenges. Mark and I are always setting goals that challenge us. We always say, "The purpose of setting a really big goal is not so that you can achieve it so much, but it's who you become in the process of achieving it." A friend of mine, Jim Rohn, says, "You want to set goals big enough so that in the process of achieving them you become someone worth being."

I think that to be a millionaire is nice but so what? People make the money and then they lose it. People get the big houses and then they burn down, or Silicon Valley goes belly up and all of a sudden they don't have a big house anymore. But who you became in the process of learning how to do that can never be taken away from you. So what we do is constantly put big challenges in front of us.

We have a book called *Chicken Soup for the Teacher's Soul.* (You'll have to make sure to get a copy for your wife.) I was a teacher and a teacher trainer for years. But because of the success of the *Chicken Soup* books I haven't been in the education world that much. I've got to go out and relearn how do I market to that world? I met with a Superintendent of Schools. I met with a guy named Jason Dorsey who's one of the number one consultants in the world in that area. I found out who has the best selling book in that area. I sat down with his wife for a day and talked about her marketing approaches.

I believe that if you face any kind of adversity, whether losing your job, your spouse dies, you get divorced, you're in an accident like Christopher Reeves and become paralyzed, or whatever, you simply do what you have to do. You find out who's already handled the problem and how did they've handled it. Then you get the support you need to get through it by their example. Whether it's a counselor in your church or you go on a retreat or you read the Bible, you do something that gives you the support you need to get to the other end.

You also have to know what the end is that you want to have. Do you want to be remarried? Do you just want to have a job and be a single mom? What is it? If you reach out and ask for support I think you'll get help. People really like to help other people. They're not always available because sometimes they're going through problems also; but there's always someone with a helping hand.

Often I think we let our pride get in the way. We let our stubbornness get in the way. We let our belief in how the world should be interfere and get in our way instead of dealing with how the world is. When we get that out of that way then we can start doing that which we need to do to get where we need to go.

Wright

If you could have a platform and tell our audience something you feel that would help or encourage them, what would you say?

Canfield

I'd say number one is to believe in yourself, believe in your dreams, and trust your feelings. I think too many people are trained wrong when they're little kids. For example, when kids are mad at their daddy they're told, "You're not mad at your Daddy."

They say, "Gee, I thought I was."

Or the kid says, "That's going to hurt," and the doctor says, "No it's not." Then they give you the shot and it hurts. They say, "See that didn't hurt, did it?" When that happened to you as a kid, you started to not trust yourself.

You may have asked your mom, "Are you upset?" and she says, "No," but she really was. So you stop learning to trust your perception.

I tell this story over and over. There are hundreds of people I've met who've come from upper class families where they make big incomes and the dad's a doctor. The kid wants to be a mechanic and work in an auto shop because that's what he loves. The family says, "That's beneath us. You can't do that." So the kid ends up being an anesthesiologist killing three people because he's not paying attention. What he really wants to do is tinker with cars. I tell people you've got to trust your own feelings, your own motivations, what turns you on, what you want to do, what makes you feel good, and quit worrying about what other people say, think, and want for you.

Decide what you want for yourself and then do what you need to do to go about getting it. It takes work.

I read a book a week minimum and at the end of the year I've read fifty-two books. We're talking about professional books—books on self-help, finances, psychology, parenting, and so forth. At the end of ten years I've read 520 books. That puts me in the top 1 percent of people knowing important information in this country. But most people are spending their time watching television.

When I went to work for W. Clement Stone, he told me, "I want you to cut out one hour a day of television."

"Okay," I said, "what do I do with it?"

"Read," he said.

He told me what kind of books to read. He said, "At the end of a year you'll have spent 365 hours reading. Divide that by a forty-hour work week and that's nine and a half weeks of education every year."

I thought, "Wow, that's two months." It was like going back to summer school.

As a result of his advice I have close to 8,000 books in my library. The reason I'm involved in this book project instead of someone else is that people like me, Jim Rohn, Les Brown, and you read a lot. We listen to tapes and we go to seminars. That's why we're the people with the information.

I always say that your raise becomes effective when you do. You'll become more effective as you gain more skills, more insight, and more knowledge.

Wright

Jack, I have watched your career for over a decade and your accomplishments are just outstanding. But your humanitarian efforts are really what impress me. I think that you're doing great things not only in California, but all over the country.

Canfield

It's true. In addition to all of the work we do, we pick one to three charities and we've given away over six million dollars in the last eight years, along with our publisher who matches every penny we give away. We've planted over a million trees in Yosemite National Park. We've bought hundreds of thousands of cataract operations in third world countries. We've contributed to the Red Cross, the Humane Society, and on it goes. It feels like a real blessing to be able to make that kind of a contribution to the world.

Wright

Today we have been talking with Jack Canfield, founder and co-creator of the *Chicken Soup for the Soul* book series. As of 2006, there are sixty-five titles and eighty million copies in print in over thirty-seven languages.

Canfield

The most recent book is *The Success Principles*. In it I share sixty-four principles that other people and I have utilized to achieve great levels of success.

In 2002 we published *Chicken Soup for the Soul of America*. It includes stories that grew out of 9/11 and is a real healing book for our nation. I would encourage readers to get a copy and share it with their families.

Wright

I will stand in line to get one of those. Thank you so much being with us on *Speaking of Success.*

About The Author

JACK CANFIELD is one of America's leading experts on developing self-esteem and peak performance. A dynamic and entertaining speaker, as well as a highly sought-after trainer, he has a wonderful ability to inform and inspire audiences toward developing their own human potential and personal effectiveness.

Jack Canfield is most well-known for the *Chicken Soup for the Soul* series, which he co-authored with Mark Victor Hansen, and for his audio programs about building high self-esteem. Jack is the founder of Self-Esteem Seminars, located in Santa Barbara, California, which trains entrepreneurs, educators, corporate leaders, and employees how to accelerate the achievement of their personal and professional goals. Jack is also the founder of The Foundation for Self Esteem, located in Culver City, California, which provides self-esteem resources and training to social workers, welfare recipients, and human resource professionals.

Jack graduated from Harvard in 1966, received his ME degree at the university of Massachusetts in 1973, and earned an Honorary Doctorate from the University of Santa Monica. He has been a high school and university teacher, a workshop facilitator, a psychotherapist, and a leading authority in the area of self-esteem and personal development.

As a result of his work with prisoners, welfare recipients, and inner-city youth, Jack was appointed by the state legislature to the California Task Force to Promote Self-Esteem and Personal and Social Responsibility. He also served on the board of trustees of the National Council for Self-Esteem.

Jack Canfield
Worldwide Headquarters
The Jack Canfield Companies
P.O. Box 30880
Santa Barbara, CA 93130
Phone: 805.563.2935
Fax: 805.563.2945
www.jackcanfield.com

Chapter 8

LINDA SHERWIN

THE INTERVIEW

David Wright (Wright)

Linda is an internationally published author who works with leaders to help them improve performance and productivity in their organization. Through her keynotes, seminars, and consulting, Linda teaches her clients how to connect and communicate more powerfully to improve relationships and increase the bottom line. With over twenty-five years of corporate and theatrical experience, Linda delivers dynamic presentations that get results. She is a member of the National Speakers Association, the International Federation for Professional Speakers, and is the current president of the Florida Speakers Association.

As a speaker and an author, your message is all about performing better and motivating others to be more productive. Tell us, how did you get into this? And why do you do what you do?

Linda Sherwin (Sherwin)

Working and consulting with a variety of companies I was shocked to see so many people unhappy at work, not fulfilled in their lives, experiencing failure, and not getting back up and not knowing what they could do to help themselves. I found myself talking to these people, helping them to find their passion, helping them to get through the dilemma, and helping them to be the best they could be. I realized these were not simple, isolated cases but almost an epidemic in corporate America.

I also realized it came down to their relationship with the leaders of the organization. How passionate were their leaders in what they were doing? And were they able to communicate that passion to their employees? Most often they were not. When they communicated with their staff they talked *at* them—there was no connection. What was missing was the "sizzle" to the "steak." There was no pizzazz to their communication. They could talk the facts but there was no drawing in of their audience, no performance. Most people simply didn't know how and, as with most things unknown, especially about public speaking, there was the fear factor. And so the "fearless performance expert" was born.

Wright

That's quite a tag line Linda. What does a fearless performance expert do?

Sherwin

It's all about effective communication. No matter where we are in our business lives we are communicating with other people for any number of reasons. Whether as the CEO you are announcing the quarterly results and the business plan moving forward or as a Director presenting your budget to the Board or as a Manager explaining to your team about the need to meet a critical deadline, the most successful leaders master powerful communication and know how to get every employee on board. You may say, "Oh well, people do that all the time and their message gets across." Yes, the message may be heard but is it accepted and acted upon with the enthusiasm and commitment that is required to really make it work?

I have watched the employees of a large organization as the CEO reports quarterly results and the attitude of most of the people is, "So what does that do for me?" They're not motivated to be part of the solution and so in reality they can possibly become part of the problem. When a leader speaks in such a way that the audience, whoever that might be, is inspired by the presentation of the words and motivated to be in agreement with the speaker, there is immediate buy-in and incredible results. A lot of leaders don't know how to do this effectively, whether it's based on fear or they just don't have a process to learn how, they don't do it. Then they wonder why they are not getting the results they want from their people.

Wright

Share with us how this strategy has worked in your own life and in the lives of your clients.

Sherwin

As well as being a corporate consultant, I have been an actor, primarily in the theater. Call it a hobby, call it a passion. The skills that I have mastered to be effective on stage and connect with the audience are the same skills I use today in working with my CEOs and top business leaders to connect with their people and run successful companies. The connections and similarities of the actor on stage and leadership in business are profound.

As an actor it is your job to convince the audience that you are the character you are portraying. You have to create the character in their minds, build the characterization, elicit the relationship you want to achieve toward that character, make the audience be interested in the character's outcome, leave the audience with a lasting impression—and entertain them—all of that in a matter of two hours. That's quite an achievement. As a leader you need your audience—your people—to see you as that leader, to have that image firmly implanted in their minds, have them understand what you are trying to achieve, what part they play in the process, and motivate them to be really enrolled in the process.

In my work as a consultant I was often the agent of change, recommending new processes or structure within an organization. A lot of my work was spent talking to the people who may be involved in the process or structure that was destined for change. It was my responsibility to learn as much as I could from these people about how things currently worked. As you know, most people do not like change. I found that being an advocate of "improvement," not necessarily "change," was very powerful in getting buy-in from people. They were not threatened by me or the questions I was asking because they saw themselves as part of the solution, and often had very good ideas about resolving the problem. I always made sure to give credit to any staff member who had an idea that I made part of the recommendations.

People want to be part of what is happening. Let's face it; most of us spend more time at our jobs than we do with family and friends. So of course we would like to have a say in what happens. Many leaders just don't get it. If you have your people on board with you—truly on board—phenomenal things can happen within the organization.

Wright

What's really the problem, Linda? Aren't leaders communicating today?

Sherwin

That's exactly the problem. Most leaders and department heads *think* they are communicating. Most leaders think they are connecting with their people. They think they are effective. They don't know they have a problem. They think their people are happy. They think their people are coming to work fulfilled. In corporate America, 87 percent of the people would quit their job today if they could—87 percent! That means 87 percent are unfulfilled. What kind of productivity is that creating in the workforce today?

What my programs do first and foremost is pose awareness. Then we can get working on correction.

Wright

So if that's reality, what can be done about it? And more specifically, how does your program solve this lack of communication?

Sherwin

We go beyond communication. We strive for connection. There is a difference between what you say or send in your message and what people receive. In any organization we have to start at the top. It's imperative that the leaders communicate effectively with their people, their clients, and with each other. Leaders may be communicating what they want to say, but they are not focused on how it is being heard so that the people receiving the message truly get it. There are different levels of communication.

A leader is most effective in their communications when they use total body communication. That means everything: facial expressions, body language, as well as the words they use. Studies have shown, and I'm sure you know, that most of our communication is non-verbal. It's not just what we say, but how we say it. Actors, particularly stage actors, must use body language extensively to portray their characters. Today with the global economy it becomes even more important that we recognize and be aware of what our total body communication may mean to another culture. We use these same techniques, honed over years of effective use in the theater, to create total body communication for our client. We come into the organization and help the leaders create their own communication style that is effective, authentic, practical, and probably most importantly immediately applicable.

Wright

That's a unique approach. Give us some examples of how your communication techniques have caused connection in the workforce.

Sherwin

Well, let's talk about my client Rob. We used the theatrical technique of sense memory to help him become effective in his presentations. He felt he was not connecting with his people. He was an excellent speaker with great content, but something was just not working. Here's a man who knows his material in and out but get him in front of an audience and there was just no rapport. You might say he had the "steak" but no "sizzle."

We helped him shift that by using his sense memory to physically recreate within him the feelings and emotions of an event where he was truly connecting with an audience. Then we found a single word declaration to bring those sensations back instantly when he needed them to relive it in a total body communication. It was most interesting and his words to me were, "This is profound and powerful!" And that's step number one to our communication course—passion.

Wright

Is success as simple as finding your passion and following it?

Sherwin

It's the first step. Now let me ask you something, do you know of one successful person who is not passionate about what he or she is doing? Passion is vital to success. It is as simple as finding your passion, but finding your passion is not that simple. People are not passionate about what they do because they don't really know what it is they want to do, and they don't know what they want to do because they don't know who they are. Once you know who you are, the character of "you," and how to be that character, you're off to a great start. Be the character and the passion will reveal itself.

Wright

After the leader taps into his or her passion, what's the next step to ensure powerful communication?

Sherwin

Finding the purpose. It's all about enrollment. Enrollment is more than just talking someone into something. It's about connecting with that person in such a way that he or she is truly inspired and motivated to see what you see and buy into being part of it. Actors on stage enroll the audience in the story they are creating and the audience lives through it with them. How often have you attended a play and have totally forgotten that you were in the audience? That fourth wall disappears and you are a part of the events on the stage. That's connection.

In an organization, it's important to enroll others to see how their purpose fits into the company's big picture. If everyone in the company moved on purpose and was playing his or her role in the big picture vision, how would that company produce? When the individual's purpose is a part of the organization's purpose you have a win–win. And most leaders don't get this. It's not just talking at your people, and not just communicating, no matter how passionate you may be. You can have all the passion in the world but if no one else is on board—if the people are not enrolled—nothing will happen.

And that is the situation in so many organizations today in corporate America. People may participate but not to the extent and not to the level of success the leaders are looking for. It's important to truly enroll them in the corporate vision. It's all about enrolling the people and ensuring everybody on the team is fulfilling their own unique purpose. They have to see their purpose in the role they play. And show up every day, passionate about what they're going to do.

My focus is to help the leaders communicate better, to have their passion for the organization felt by their people and for their people to be enrolled in it. Let's face it. There may be individuals who are working at something that isn't their highest choice and isn't what they really want to do. After all, sometimes you simply need a job. So how can you motivate these people who may not be doing what they really want to do to be the best they can be at what they are doing?

That's what I do. We go through exercises with the team to identify their passion and how that fits into the big picture. Get them enrolled as to how their role fits into the vision and mission of the organization. And that's working on purpose, and when everyone is on purpose what would it be like? If everyone was living and working on purpose, what would the company look like? What would it be like to come to work on Friday? What would it be like to come in on Monday? What would the people contribute? What kind of a difference could that make to the organization, to their clients and vendors, to the business industry as a whole?

Wright

What's the third step to your Powerful Communication Course?

Sherwin

David, there has to be an element of play. Why is our connotation of work something negative? Can you imagine an organization encouraging an element of play in the work day? Just think of how we perceive play. It's positive, enjoyable, and something we want to do. Most work environments today are not conducive to play. This answers the age old question, "Where is the playfulness in my day?" I think it would be hard to be creative and passionate without some element of play, without feeling, as a psychologist would say, the child in you again. There has to be some fun there. You say "fun" in corporate America and there are visions of everyone running around crazy, not being productive, and yet the opposite is true.

My son is an art director at an advertising agency, and when I ask him how is work going he says, "It's not work Mom, I love what I do." Organizations that work really well are organizations where that element of play is not just tolerated, it's encouraged. It provides a balance to the work day. A little levity in the workplace can do wonders to boost morale and productivity.

Now, defining the play can be a challenge. As you look at the diverse generations we now have in the workplace, what constitutes play? Millennials are our future. Millennials are those born between 1980 and 2000, and how they see the world and respond to it is different than the Boomers or the Generation Xers. (Of course that's another whole topic.) But organizations must keep in mind that if they want to exist in the global economy and in the future, they need to understand and be mindful of the various generational mindsets, particularly the Millennials. Let me tell you, they are all about purpose, passion, and play.

Think of the theater: "the play's the thing" (Shakespeare's *Hamlet*). You've done all the work—the rehearsals, the actors have made their connections and found their characters' passion. Whether it's a drama or a comedy, you have to enroll the audience in what you are up to. The actors perform the play and look at the message the audience gets. And sometimes the message resonates with them for a long time.

I don't know if you saw the show the *Phantom of the Opera,* when it first opened over twenty years ago, or if you were one of the over eighty million people worldwide who have seen it. But if you simply hear the music today, you'll remember the magnificence of it. Everything comes back to you.

I think that's what we are up to in business. How do we relive the magnificence of our purpose and passion? And that's what play does for us.

Just last week I was walking into the office of one of my clients where I had done a team-building workshop. One of the people came up to me, greeted me, and gave me a great big hug—and that workshop was three years ago. We had created such a connection among the team members with that element of play, that it's still there—even when they saw me after some time had passed.

Wright

Let's say a company went through your communication course and adhered to the principles. What would the business look like in eighteen months to two years?

Sherwin

First of all, the bottom line of the organization would be improved. Leaders would communicate with integrity and candor both among themselves and with their people and that would eventually evolve to employees communicating with each other—with their peers. Within the organization, you would know that people would be speaking with authenticity and honesty. There would be no second-guessing of what was going on—no hidden messages. You know how time-consuming that can be. You say to yourself, "What are they really saying? Do they mean that or do they mean this?" You know that if you hear something and know it is straightforward and honest, you can respond from your honesty.

I believe that today in corporate America people have stopped trusting. If you think someone is coming from a hidden agenda, then you come from your hidden agenda and the whole thing becomes very contrived, and very false. But if you know that the person is speaking with honesty, you respond with honesty and a lot more gets accomplished a lot faster. I believe the productivity of each employee would improve by at least 15 percent, which would eventually translate to a bottom line improvement as well.

Secondly, the employees would be passionate, enrolled, and fulfilled and would realize their roles in the organization. I mentioned earlier that some surveys have found that 87 percent of Americans don't like their jobs. A recent article in *Forbes* magazine reported that it costs the nation an estimated $150 billion—with a "b"—$150 *billion* per year in treatment for stress related problems, absenteeism, reduced productivity, and employee turnover. How could we radically shift that number? What if people were passionate about what they were doing? What if people felt less stress and were more excited to come to work?

Every employee would feel connected in the big vision and know their part in creating and maintaining it. People would be closer to discovering their own passion so they could give 110 percent. On a day-to-day basis, when people are passionate about what they are doing, they do it the best they can. They work more efficiently because they know they are making a contribution. They are coming up with new ideas for improvements because they know in the end it is something good for them and how they do their jobs. They know that management and leadership are open to suggestions. With every employee producing at peak performance, this would instantaneously improve the bottom line. When you and your position are a perfect fit, it's magic. And the rest is easy.

Thirdly, can you imagine being a client or a customer of an organization like this? What would it be like doing business with people who are all communicating and connecting and doing business with people who want you, the client, to have a memorable experience with them and their company? Do you think you would feel good doing business with these people? Do you think you as the client would build a relationship and have loyalty to the organization? Absolutely.

People at all levels would be exceeding expectations because they would be in tune with the organization. It's like the play you go to and you come out singing one of the songs you heard. You are remembering the message. That's what it is—creating a company that is prosperous and productive; you have people who are on purpose, people who love to come into work, who know that they are making a contribution, know that they are an integral part of the organization and not just simply workers there. Just think of it: people connecting with people, improved communications leader-to-leader, and leaders to their people, employees to each other, employees to the customer. It's magnificent. You have a company with a productive work environment, an improved bottom line, passionate and involved employees, and happy, loyal clients. You have a hit company. And just like a hit Broadway play it never goes away.

Wright

I believe you're serious about this.

Sherwin

Oh, I am serious about this. I get very excited. I get very passionate about it.

Wright

As I was trying to ferret out the things to learn here today, it occurred to me that if I am passionate about something, my people don't necessarily get it, do they?

Sherwin

Not necessarily. You have to be able to take your passion and enroll your people in it. I've worked with CEOs who were very passionate about what they were doing but they couldn't get that passion over to their people. They couldn't get the people involved because they were not enrolling them; they were not getting their people to see their part in the big picture—their part in the passion.

Wright

What an interesting topic and what an interesting conversation. I've learned a lot here today and I'm sure our readers will. I really appreciate your taking all this time with me to answer these questions. Thank you so much for being here and teaching this important lesson.

Sherwin

Thank you, David.

About the Author

LINDA SHERWIN is a business consultant who works with leaders to help them connect and communicate with confidence to improve performance and productivity in their organizations. Known for her passionate presentation style and high energy, she teaches her clients how to increase productivity, attract loyal customers, retain involved employees, and improve the bottom line by encouraging authentic communication at all levels of the organization.

Whether listening to a keynote, working through the Powerful Performance eCourses, attending a Standing Ovation retreat, or being coached exclusively one-on-one in the Platinum Executive Coaching program, her clients transform themselves from traumatic to dramatic presenters. Her unique process and readily applicable techniques get results fast! Discover how you can connect and communicate with authenticity and integrity and get the results you want from your people and your business.

Linda Sherwin
Sherwin Enterprises Inc.
1314 E. Las Olas Blvd., PMB 707
Fort Lauderdale, FL 33301
Phone: 954.536.1813
E-mail: Linda@LindaSherwin.com
www.LindaSherwin.com

Chapter 9

Gary Mull

THE INTERVIEW

David Wright (Wright)

Today we are talking with Gary Mull. As a professional speaker, keynote presenter, and seminar leader, Gary has delivered his entertaining and informative talks before thousands in government, civic, and professional groups internationally. He has written many published articles and has been a guest and host of several television talk shows. His new book, *Set Your Sail for Success,* distills life lessons from his lifelong passion for sailing.

Gary has earned the honor of Distinguished Toastmaster, Toastmasters International's highest award, and currently serves the organization as International Director. He holds degrees in Business Administration, Management, and Organizational Development, Education, and Nutrition, as well as several professional certifications, including Microsoft Certified Systems Engineer and Certified Trainer. Gary is a charter member of the Professional Speakers Guild and member of the U.S. Coast Guard Auxiliary.

Gary, welcome to *Speaking of Success.*

Gary Mull (Mull)

Thank you, it's good to be here.

Wright

In your view, how does someone become a success?

Mull

I don't know that one necessarily *becomes* a success. I think that's a misnomer. Success is an event not a person. Rather, you can become *successful,* and if you look at the breakdown of that word, someone successful is someone who is full of success or is somebody who has achieved many successes. Successful events actually are milestones that come as part of a successful life, so it is not really the events themselves, but the *process* of continually setting and achieving goals that makes us successful.

By the same token I think that to call somebody a *failure* is also inaccurate. A failure is not a person. A failure is an event, and in fact, it's only by going through failures that you ultimately become successful.

Success isn't permanent and neither is failure fatal. The only way to be successful is to draw on experiences we've had—both good and bad. Many people are afraid of failure. I think one should embrace failures, and the concepts that are learned from them because it is the path to success.

Wright

What have been some of the influences on your life that have shaped your thinking or helped you to become successful?

Mull

I had a lot of good influences on me growing up that helped instill good values. I also value my early boating, camping, and culinary experiences as a kid because I had a tightly-knit extended family—parents, grandparents, aunts, and uncles—who provided me with love, support, and great opportunities to learn and grow. My Dad taught me the value of consistency, steadfastness, and integrity. Mom taught me benevolence and courage—to reach beyond myself and take risks. By the way, when I was a child, she was a housewife. She then went back to school and got her BA and master's degrees, and now has a successful career.

I also value my church experiences and the values my faith instilled.

My military experience taught me a lot as well. I served in the Air Force in a wide array of assignments and locations, which helped hone my flexibility and discipline, including my education, both formal, and continuing. Not only do I have several degrees and certifications, but over the years, I've studied the philosophies of hundreds of the most successful people in history.

I've had my share of stormy seas in life, but I am thankful for the many good influences I've had.

Wright

Gary, many of your ideas are expressed through the analogy of sailing. How did you first get interested in sailing as a way to analogize life concepts?

Mull

I started my interest in sailing as a very young boy. I grew up in the "Great Lake State" of Michigan so of course, surrounded by water and boating opportunities, it was a natural fit. I started sailing at summer camp and in years after, decided to go to a camp specifically focused on sailing where we actually camped out on an island for a few weeks. I also wound up teaching sailing as a camp counselor. I developed a love for it through those experiences.

There's really nothing like being on a sailboat. You harness the natural forces and hear the wind in the sails and the slap of the water against the hull. It's just something I fell in love with and have continued to love through out my life. I realized early on that sailing was life and the rest was just details. Eventually, I realized that many of the principals that lead to success in sailing are also useful for becoming successful in life.

Wright

What are some of the key concepts that you talk about in your keynote presentations?

Mull

Well, I have several presentations that I give: "Leadership Secrets of Captain Bly," which focuses on leadership concepts, "Voyage to New Horizons," where we discuss risk-taking, and I have several other presentations.

The main presentation that seems to be the most popular and the one I enjoy the most is "Set Your Sails for Success." In it I draw on a lifetime of sailing experiences and talk about some of the analogies that can be made from sailing to life.

There are many things, obviously, about the sailing experience that you can't control that are very much like life: You can't control the wind. You can't control the waves. You can't control the tides. You can't control the weather. Sometimes you can't even control your crew. But there are things that you *can* control, and that are directly dependent on you. You can control the set of your sail and keep a firm hand on the wheel to determine your direction. There are many actions you can take in life, just like in sailing, to increase your chances of success.

One example is preparation. It's important if you're heading out on the water that you sit down and study the chart so you know how to get where you want to go. You also need to have the education to be able to read the chart effectively. There are little numbers all over a nautical chart that tell you how deep the water is, but it's not always that deep at that particular time. If you get into a place with tides, if you get into a place with currents, you need to also be able to read those things. That's very important as you prepare your journey. It's also important to know where you are as you progress. You need to either take a compass and sextant, or a Global Positioning System (GPS) that will tell you where you are. If you look at the GPS coordinates, you can tell where you are on the chart.

So obviously, right away you can see the analogy to life. We need to sit down and have a plan for life—where we are, and where we want to go. In fact, that's how I became a professional speaker. I sat down with a goal-setting program and assessed my strengths and interests and how I could best use them to help others. Some other examples are integrity, communication, attitude, and courage—all important concepts that can easily be illustrated by the sailing experience.

Wright

How does proper preparation insure a successful outcome?

Mull

Well, I don't think it *insures* a successful outcome. There are no guarantees in life. No matter what you do it's a risk; but I think it can certainly *help* you in getting a successful outcome. Preparation is very key to whatever you do. Most people probably spend more time planning a two-week vacation than they do planning their lives.

I think it's important that you plan out the different aspects of your life. For each goal that you set, you need to take into account the effect that it will have on the other goals in your life. You can't isolate your planning to one area.

For example, if I decide to sail to a certain port on the other side of Lake Erie, I had better not plan to make a stop in Chicago on the way. A sailboat only goes so fast—we go about seven knots, normally, in our thirty-three-foot Morgan, which is a big floating camper basically. We're not going to win any races in the America's Cup, so we have to pick our destination port carefully and stick to it.

In life, you may decide that you want to start and run your own business, but if you do, you need to be prepared for the sacrifices that come along the way. In other words, before you decide on a goal in one particular area of your life, you need to take the other areas into account—your family, spiritual, financial, and other goals. You need to make sure that they don't conflict with each other. Even on the fastest boat there are only so many places you can go in a given period of time.

Also, when you take time to prepare to go to a certain place, you can plan for what you need to take and the skills you need. If you're sailing in cold waters you need to take warmer equipment. If you're sailing in warmer waters you don't need to take so much weather equipment, and if you're sailing far from shore you need to stock up on more provisions and so on. When the storm hits, it's too late to return to shore for your weather gear.

It's the same in life. If you take the time to determine your goals so that you know where you are going and can make that plan on how to get there, then you'll be prepared along the way. And sure, things are going to change, but if you're as prepared as possible for the inevitable and the surprise elements that will crop up, you're going to be more successful, or at least you will have a better chance at success.

Wright

There are very good life questions that people need to ask themselves: Where is it that you want to go? Do you want to be President of the United States or do you want to be a carpenter or a plumber?

Mull

That's right, and whatever it is that you want to do, there are steps you need to take to get you there. When you sail, you continue to take steps to keep on the course that you've set. In life, we need to do the same things. When we form good habits and continually perform them, we can't help but be successful. The first and most important step is to decide what you want and find out how to get there.

Wright

What kind of preparations should be made to be successful in life?

Mull

First of all, it starts with education. I think your education is key. I mentioned earlier that you need to know what those numbers mean on your chart. It's important that you get the proper education to give context to your life experience. Get a good technical education for the things you want to do.

I think you also need to continue an overall education process on *why* things work. There are many people in the world who know *how,* but not a lot of people who know *why* things work. If you know *why,* I think you'll be much more successful.

Formal education is important, but so is continuing to read books in your field, spend time talking with successful people, test out new ideas, and so on. It's vital to know the charts and be able to read them, but you also need to know the procedures for navigating, and what to do to save your skin and your crew in case a storm blows up. Most importantly, though, I think you prepare for big challenges by taking on small challenges. Even if those ventures end in failure, the knowledge and experience you gain will help you in future endeavors.

Wright

Why is the analogy of sailing such a great way to illustrate the key concepts in your book?

Mull

I think that sailing has a lot of aspects to it that illustrate abstract points very well. For example, let's talk about something as abstract as integrity. What exactly is integrity, and how can you describe it? I like to relate it to the experience of being on the water. When you set out on water in a boat, one of the first things you will think about is does your boat have integrity? Is it going to spring a leak when you're out in the middle of the water and send you down to Davy Jones' locker?

My boat weighs about fifteen tons with fuel and water tanks filled, and with the equipment plus the weight of the boat itself, there is a lot of downward pressure. It's important that the integrity of the hull is maintained. If there is a small leak, the crack may be very small, but the water's going to flow in and it will sink.

Obviously this is a good analogy because it illustrates the calamity that can happen when there's a breach in our integrity. There's a lot of downward pressure in life, too—a lot of negative—you just open the newspaper any time and try to find some positive news in there, or on television. It's a challenge. So it's vital to maintain that integrity. Even the smallest crack can wind up sinking our boat. This is quite evident when we put it in those terms, while it may be difficult to understand in the abstract.

Another good example is *courage*. It takes courage to go out on the water, as it does to do make some of the hard choices in life. It's a great analogy. We can have all the knowledge in the world, but if we don't have the courage to take risks we won't get anywhere. We have all heard that a boat is safer in the harbor, but that's not what boats are made for. A boat is made to be properly maintained and to be taken out and enjoyed. Besides that, I don't believe that boats are safer in the harbor at all. I know that if I leave my boat alone in the dock for very long, the spiders and the seagulls are going to "decorate" it for me, and leave me a mess to clean up when I come back. If I leave it alone for a whole season, the varnish will peel, the wood starts to rot, and rust and corrosion will start to develop on the metal parts. Eventually, if it's left unused, it will become unusable.

I think the human mind and body are the same way. Life is a ship meant to be sailed—to go out and venture. You may think it is safer not to take risks, to sit at home and watch television instead of joining a Toastmasters Club or taking a computer class. But that's not what human beings are designed for. If you "take your mind out for a sail," you're going to be more successful, you'll actually live longer and last longer and be happier in your life. Now, you could tell somebody to go out and take some risks in life, but when you give the illustration of how exhilarating and exciting it is to be sailing across the water, rather than tied to the pier, I think it resonates much more.

Wright

Is sailing a better analogy that power boating?

Mull

Absolutely! The boat analogy is great all the way around, but I think sailing is a better analogy because of the fact that you're dealing more directly with the elements, and you need to gain a bit more skill to harness the elements to get where you want to go. In power boating you pretty much pick your spot, hit the throttle, and off you go. But with sailing, it makes a great analogy for life because there are so many things about the sailing experience that you can't control. You have to rely on your skills and your wits and the techniques you've developed over time to harness the natural forces to get where you want to go.

In life it's the same thing. You may have a good start or a bad start. You may encounter difficulties. Some people have higher challenges than others, some people may have an easier path, but all in all, when it comes down to it, the success that you find in life has much more to do with the skills that you've developed and your willingness and motivation to set a proper sail to get where you want to go. The very winds that hold you back or drive you onto the rocks are the same winds that will drive you to where you want to go, if you know how to properly set your sails.

This is an important concept to grasp—*regardless of which direction the wind blows, you can set your sail in any direction.* If the wind is blowing from the starboard or port sides (that's right and left for "landlubbers") it's easy to sail along. The key is to trim the sail to get the most effective use of it. Of course I'm talking about the concept of continuous improvement, Dr. Deming's philosophy. If the wind is behind you, you can set your sails on a "wing on wing" formation and go with the wind. That's the fastest and most fun way to sail, but it's also the most dangerous because the wind can change. If you're not careful, your boom is way beyond you outside of your control. If you get off course a little bit that wind can whip that boom across the boat and if you're not careful it can boom you right in the head and knock you overboard. A lot of boats have been sunk that way. A lot of people have been injured that way.

It can be the same in life. You have winds prevailing in a certain direction, but those winds can change without notice. Even if you pick the proper way to set your sails you can't just go down into the cabin and take a nap. You have to pay attention. You have to insure that you're watching the weather and watching the clouds. That translates to watching the trends and the economy in life and your education.

Otherwise that boom can quickly zip across and crack you in the head.

There are many people who have a chosen career and for some reason that career is no longer viable or the opportunity at a company where they chose to work no longer exists for them, so they go into depression or wind up in a tough financial situation because they have a hard time transitioning.

If you take the analogy of sailing you know you're going to have wind changes all the time. It's not good, and it's not bad. It just is. It may be inconvenient and downright painful, but you can't change it by standing on the bow cursing the elements. You've got to set your sails and if the wind changes you've got to set your sails in a different direction.

Wright

Looking at this sailing as being analogous to life, I've got friends who sail and of course they tell me that you can even go in the opposite direction from the wind. What about those times when there is no wind?

Mull

If you want to sail east and the wind is blowing from the east, obviously you can't sail into the wind. You're going to have to *tack* a little bit. By this I mean that you sail a little bit to the northeast and a little bit to the southeast and so on, and eventually you'll get east where you want to go, even if the wind is blowing directly against you.

Again, this is a very important life concept. Most of us can't walk in and ask for the CEO's job or start our own company making a million dollars a year. The wind is too strong against us. We have to tack. We might take on a starting position at a company in a field we are interested in, get some additional education, partner with someone who has skills or financing that we need, take a course of study, and so on—something that will take us in the direction of our goals without trying to sail directly into the wind.

You also have some times when you look at the weather and you think, "Hey this is going to be a great sailing day" and you get out there on the water and find there is just no wind at all. In that case I guess you just have to learn patience. In reality, you can create a little wind by rocking the boat back and forth and it will create a little bit of movement forward. Most of the time though, I use that time to re-examine the charts, do some maintenance on board, and be thankful that I brought enough provisions with me from my last port to last through the journey. See the life analogy there? Eventually some wind is going to come along, and even with just a little bit of wind, if you trim the sails right, what little bit of wind there is will get you going. Pretty soon it picks up and you'll be on your way again.

Wright

Most of us who are in business, especially management or business ownership, look for the calm.

Mull

There are advantages to calm, and of course we hope for it—times when the wind is fair and steady and the waves are small. But keep in mind that first of all, you don't want it too calm or you may not be getting anywhere. You make more progress when the winds are stronger. Also, most importantly, you can't *make* it calm, so rather than prepare for calm seas and hope for the best, prepare for the *rough* seas and hope for the best.

Fair winds and seas can lull us into complacency and it's vital that even in ideal conditions we continue to plan and prepare for the journey ahead, and the potential storms.

Wright

What were some of the most memorable events on your 2,000-mile journey from the Gulf coast to Michigan?

Mull

That's a great question; I have so many of them. My wife and I took our time coming up the coast—about four months—and it was really nice. We saw so many interesting things along the way. We had dinner at the Vanderbilt Manson in New York coming up the Hudson River. (That's a bit of an inside joke. Actually, they've turned the grounds into a public park and we grilled bratwurst out behind it.) Another stop along the Hudson River was to tour West Point. Another highlight of the trip was a serendipitous stop at a little isolated island in the middle of the Chesapeake called Tangier Island. We went to Annapolis during graduation and got to see all the midshipmen in uniform, and a performance by the Blue Angels, right above the boat.

There is so much heritage to be explored and learned from, if you take the time, and so many interesting sights like the lighthouses on

Cape Hatteras, the Cotton Exchange in Savannah, Atlantic City, Cape May in New Jersey, and even the "yellow brick road" commemorating the author of the Wizard of Oz in New York.

Speaking of New York, one of the most memorable experiences I had was actually sailing underneath the Statue of Liberty. What made it even more meaningful was the fact that we traveled through New York Harbor on the Memorial Day immediately following 9/11. There were dozens of Navy and Coast Guard ships that had come out for the events.

Another great aspect was that we got to visit with family and friends along the way. All along the coast we would call people and tell them to come out to the boat. We would go out for a little bit and come back to port. This was a great time to visit with people and share that experience. Not only was it a great life experience, but it gave me a lifetime of speaking material and entertaining stories to share with others.

Wright

What excites you the most about sharing your message with others?

Mull

I like what I call The Light Bulb Effect. I like to talk to folks and see that symbolic light bulb come on above their heads. They're dealing with an issue perhaps, whether it is in the office or their home life or personal life, and you can tell when you have shed a different philosophy on things that cuts though the fog like the lighthouse beacon in the night.

When people find information in my message that can be useful to them to apply to their situation, and perhaps help them to change their whole lives, that's when I feel most fulfilled. I get many cards, letters, and people coming up to me to tell me how much they enjoyed my materials or how much they have gotten out of it. That means a lot. But I especially enjoy seeing it on their faces when they start to "get it." To me, that's what it's really all about—helping other people to succeed.

Wright

In addition to your keynotes, you also do leadership development and communication training. How well do the precepts you talk about in your keynotes fit in with the concept of leadership?

Mull

Well, I believe they are vital to leadership. As a matter of fact, if you look at the things that make a good leader, number one I think is a positive attitude. In sailing we talk about the various winds that blow and setting your sails for success, and the proper attitude is paramount in leadership. Charting a proper course and being able to communicate both the vision and the optimism to your crew are vital to leadership.

Also, preparation is very important. As a leader it is vital to make sure that as an organization you're prepared for what comes up. Having the courage to step out and take some of the risks is important to achieving success. We talk about risk and reward in business, which is very important.

I think that integrity is very, very important. In fact, there is a lot of news lately illustrating the lack of integrity of a few prominent leaders in corporate America and politics. I would say the vast majority doesn't fall under that category, but the few who do seem to find the limelight or the limelight finds them and we can see the destruction because of it.

All of those precepts are not just desirable *leadership* qualities, but desirable *human* qualities, and they are vital to being a successful leader, so it fits quite well.

I've partnered with some really outstanding people in an organization called The Optibility Performance Group, focusing on leadership and communication development training and consulting. It's been a great way to positively impact people and organizations and help them to be successful.

Wright

You've spoken to hundreds of people employed by Fortune 500 companies and small businesses alike. What kinds of issues do you find that are universal among them?

Mull

I think that ultimately, even though our individual challenges are quite separate and divergent among people and organizations, many of them boil down to some of the challenges. For example, you may have a specific problem that deals with integrity. You may need to make tough decisions, especially as a leader, that not everybody's going to like. Whether that decision is to shut down an operation that's not doing well or whether it's to turn in a fellow employee who's doing something to harm himself (or herself) or the organization. Whatever that decision is, ultimately you have to come back to your own value system and determine what the right thing to do is.

Another constant is courage. If you don't have the courage to step out and take some risks you're not going to find the success that you seek. Preparation, attitude, communication, and so on, all the concepts I talk about are pretty universal. If you use stories and examples, problems and challenges that other people have faced, and analogies that can bring the point home and make them memorable, it helps people to face and overcome their specific challenges.

Wright

What a great conversation Gary. I really appreciate your taking all this time with me this morning to answer all these questions. I've learned a lot and I've got a lot to think about here. Our readers will also, I suspect.

Mull

I appreciate your time as well. Thank you for the conversation. I wish you success.

About the Author

GARY MULL is an accomplished professional speaker, keynote presenter, author, and consultant. As an expert on leadership, communication, and change management issues, he is internationally known for his warmth, energy, and honesty in his motivational presentations, consultations, writing, and television appearances. Gary brings his vast life experiences and philosophies from the corporate world, high-tech industries, entrepreneurship, private business, government, sailing, world travel, and life to each client and presentation.

Gary holds degrees in Business and Administration, Management and Organizational Development, Education, and Nutrition, and several professional certifications. He is author of *Set Your Sails for Success,* a compilation of success philosophies analogized by sailing experiences.

Gary serves as International Director for Toastmasters International, and is a recipient of the organization's highest award: Distinguished Toastmaster. He is the President of the Professional Speakers Guild, a member of the U.S. Coast Guard Auxiliary, and Managing Partner of the Optibility Performance Group, an organizational development and training firm.

Gary Mull
4516 Maughn Dr.
Dayton, OH 45431
Phone: 937.252.9450
E-mail: gary@garymull
www.garymull.com

Chapter 10

DR. STEPHEN R. COVEY

THE INTERVIEW

David Wright (Wright)

We're talking today with Dr. Stephen R. Covey, cofounder and vice-chairman of Franklin Covey Company, the largest management company and leadership development organization in the world. Dr. Covey is perhaps best known as the author of *The 7 Habits of Highly Effective People* which is ranked as a number one best seller by the *New York Times*, having sold more than fourteen million copies in thirty-eight languages throughout the world. Dr. Covey is an internationally respected leadership authority, family expert, teacher, and organizational consultant. He has made teaching principle-centered living and principle-centered leadership his life's work. Dr. Covey is the recipient of the Thomas More College Medallion for Continuing Service to Humanity and has been awarded four honorary doctorate degrees. Other awards given Dr. Covey include the Sikh's 1989 International Man of Peace award, the 1994 International Entrepreneur of the Year award, *Inc.* magazine's Services Entrepreneur of the Year award, and in 1996 the National Entrepreneur of the Year Lifetime Achievement award for Entrepreneurial leadership. He has also been recognized as one of *Time* magazine's twenty-five most influential Americans and one of Sales and Marketing Management's top twenty-five power brokers. Dr. Covey earned his undergraduate degree from the University of Utah, his MBA from Harvard, and completed his doctorate at Brigham Young University. While at Brigham Young he served as assistant to the President and was also a professor of business management and organizational behavior.

Dr. Covey, welcome to *Speaking of Success!*

Dr. Stephen Covey (Covey)

Thank you.

Wright

Dr. Covey, most companies make decisions and filter them down through their organization. You, however, state that no company can succeed until individuals within it succeed. Are the goals of the company the result of the combined goals of the individuals?

Covey

Absolutely, because if people aren't on the same page, they're going to be pulling in different directions. To teach this concept, I frequently ask large audiences to close their eyes and point north, and then to keep pointing and open their eyes and they find themselves pointing all over the place. I say to them, "Tomorrow morning if you want a similar experience, ask the first ten people you meet in your organization what the purpose of your organization is and you'll find it's a very similar experience. They'll point all over the place." When people have a different sense of purpose and values, every decision that is made from then on is governed by those. There's no question that this is one of the fundamental causes of misalignment, low trust, interpersonal conflict, interdepartmental rivalry, people operating on personal agendas, and so forth.

Wright

Is that mostly a result of the inability to communicate from the top?

Covey

That's one aspect, but I think it's more fundamental. There's an inability to involve people—an unwillingness. Leaders may communicate what their mission and their strategy is, but that doesn't mean there's any emotional connection to it. Mission statements that are rushed and then announced are soon forgotten. They become nothing more than just a bunch of platitudes on the wall that mean essentially nothing and even create a source of cynicism and a sense of hypocrisy inside the culture of an organization.

Wright

How do companies ensure survival and prosperity in these tumultuous times of technological advances, mergers, downsizing, and change?

Covey

I think that it takes a lot of high trust in a culture that has something that doesn't change—principles—at its core. There are principles that people agree upon that are valued. It gives a sense of stability. Then you have the power to adapt and be flexible when you experience these kinds of disruptive new economic models or technologies that come in and sideswipe you. You don't know how to handle them unless you have something you can depend upon. If people have not agreed to a common set of principles that guide them and a common purpose, then they get their security from the outside and they tend to freeze the structure, systems, and processes inside and they cease becoming adaptable. They don't change with the changing realities of the new marketplace out there and gradually they become obsolete.

Wright

I was interested in one portion of your book *The 7 Habits of Highly Effective People* where you talk about behaviors. How does an individual go about the process of replacing ineffective behaviors with effective ones?

Covey

I think that for most people it usually requires a crisis that humbles them to become aware of their ineffective behaviors. If there's not a crisis the tendency is to perpetuate those behaviors and not change. You don't have to wait until the marketplace creates the crisis for you. Have everyone accountable on a 360 degree basis to everyone else they interact with—with feedback either formal or informal—where they are getting data as to what's happening. They will then start to realize that the consequences of their ineffective behavior require them to be humble enough to look at that behavior and to adopt new, more effective ways of doing things. Sometimes people can be stirred up to this if you just appeal to their conscience—to their inward sense of what is right and wrong. A lot of people sometimes know inwardly they're doing wrong, but the culture doesn't necessarily discourage them from continuing that. They either need feedback from people, or they need feedback from the marketplace, or they need feedback from their conscience. Then they can begin to develop a step-by-step process of replacing old habits with new, better habits.

Wright

It's almost like saying, "Let's make all the mistakes in the laboratory before we put this thing in the air."

Covey

Right; and I also think what is necessary is a paradigm shift, which is analogous to having a correct map, say of a city or of a country. If people have an inaccurate paradigm of life, of other people, and of themselves it really doesn't make much difference what their behavior or habits or attitudes are. What they need is a correct paradigm—a correct map—that describes what's going on. For instance, in the Middle Ages they used to heal people through bloodletting. It wasn't until Samuel Weiss and Pasteur and other empirical scientists discovered the germ theory that they realized for the first time they weren't dealing with the real issue. They realized why women preferred to use midwives who washed rather than doctors who didn't wash. They gradually got a new paradigm. Once you've got a new paradigm then your behavior and your attitude flows directly from it. If you have a bad paradigm or a bad map, let's say of a city, there's no way, no matter what your behavior or your habits or your attitudes are—how positive they are—you'll never be able to find the location you're looking for. This is why I believe that to change paradigms is far more fundamental than to work on attitude and behavior.

Wright

One of your seven habits of highly effective people is to begin with the end in mind. If circumstances change and hardships or miscalculation occurs, how does one view the end with clarity?

Covey

Many people think to begin with the end in mind means that you have some fixed definition of a goal that's accomplished and if changes come about you're not going to adapt to them. Instead, the "end in mind" you begin with is that you are going to create a flexible culture of high trust so that no matter what comes along you are going to do whatever it takes to accommodate that new change or that new reality and maintain a culture of high performance and high trust. You're talking more in terms of values and overall purposes that don't change, rather than specific strategies or programs that will have to change to accommodate the changing realities in the marketplace.

Wright

In this time of mistrust between people, corporations, and nations for that matter, how do we create high levels of trust?

Covey

That's a great question and it's complicated because there are so many elements that go into the creating of a culture of trust. Obviously the most fundamental one is just to have trustworthy people. But that is not sufficient because what if the organization itself is misaligned? For instance, what if you say you value cooperation but you really reward people for internal competition? Then you have a systemic or a structure problem that creates low trust inside the culture even though the people themselves are trustworthy. This is one of the insights of Edward Demming and the work he did. That's why he said that most problems are not personal; they're systemic. They're common caused. That's why you have to work on structure, systems, and processes to make sure that they institutionalize principle-centered values. Otherwise you could have good people with bad systems and you'll get bad results.

When it comes to developing interpersonal trust between people, it is made up of many, many elements such as taking the time to listen to other people, to understand them, and to see what is important to them. What we think is important to another may only be important to us, not to another. It takes empathy. You have to make and keep promises to them. You have to treat them with kindness and courtesy. You have to be completely honest and open. You have to live up to your commitments. You can't betray them behind their back. You can't badmouth them behind their back and sweet-talk them to their face. That will send out vibes of hypocrisy and it will be detected. You have to learn to apologize when you make mistakes, to admit mistakes, and to also get feedback going in every direction as much as possible. It doesn't necessarily require formal forums; it requires trust between people that will be open with each other and give each other feedback.

Wright

My mother told me to do a lot of what you're saying now, but it seems like when I got in business I simply forgot.

Covey

Sometimes we forget, but sometimes culture doesn't nurture it. That's why I say unless you work with the institutionalizing—that means formalizing into structure, systems, and processes the values—you will not have a nurturing culture. You have to constantly work on that. This is one of the big mistakes organizations make. They think trust is simply a function of being honest. That's only one small aspect. It's an important aspect, obviously, but there are so many other elements that go into the creation of a high trust culture.

Wright

"Seek first to understand then to be understood" is another of your seven habits. Do you find that people try to communicate without really understanding what other people want?

Covey

Absolutely. The tendency is to project out of our own autobiography—our own life, our own value system—onto other people, thinking we know what they want. So we don't really listen to them. We pretend to listen, but we really don't listen from within their frame of reference. We listen from within our own frame of reference and we're really preparing our reply rather than seeking to understand. This is a very common thing. In fact very few people have had any training in seriously listening. They're trained in how to read, write, and speak, but not to listen.

Reading, writing, speaking, and listening are the four modes of communication and they represent about two-thirds to three-fourths of our waking hours. About half of that time is spent listening, but it's the one skill people have not been trained in. People have had all this training in the other forms of communication. In a large audience of

1,000 people you wouldn't have more than twenty people who have had more than two weeks of training in listening. Listening is more than a skill or a technique so that you're listening within another frame of reference. It takes tremendous courage to listen because you're at risk when you listen. You don't know what's going to happen; you're vulnerable.

Wright

Sales gurus always tell me that the number one skill in selling is listening.

Covey

Yes—listening from within the customer's frame of reference. That is so true. You can see that it takes some security to do that because you don't know what's going to happen.

Wright

With our *Speaking of Success!* talk show and book we're trying to encourage people in our audience to be better, to live better, and be more fulfilled by listening to the examples of our guests. Is there anything or anyone in your life that has made a difference for you and helped you to become a better person?

Covey

I think the most influential people in my life have been my parents. I think that what they modeled was not to make comparisons and harbor jealousy or to seek recognition. They were humble people. I remember my mother one time when we were going up in an elevator and the most prominent person in the state was in the elevator. She knew him, but she spent her time talking to the elevator operator. I was just a little kid and I was so awed by this person and I said to my mom, "Why didn't you talk to the important person?" She said, "I was. I had never met him." They were really humble, modest people who were focused on service and other people rather than on themselves. I think they were very inspiring models to me.

Wright

In almost every research paper that anyone I've ever read writes about people who influenced their lives, in the top five people, three of them are teachers. My seventh grade English teacher was the greatest teacher I ever had and influenced me to no end.

Covey

Would it be correct to say that she saw in you probably some qualities of greatness you didn't even see in yourself?

Wright

Absolutely.

Covey

That's been my general experience that the key aspect of a mentor or a teacher is someone who sees in you potential that you don't even see in yourself. They treat you accordingly and eventually you come to see it in yourself. That's my definition of leadership or influence—communicating people's worth and potential so clearly that they are inspired to see it in themselves.

Wright

Most of my teachers treated me as a student, but she treated me with much more respect than that. As a matter of fact, she called me Mr. Wright in the seventh grade. I'd never been addressed by anything but a nickname. I stood a little taller; she just made a tremendous difference. Do you think there are other characteristics that mentors seem to have in common?

Covey

I think they are first of all good examples in their own personal lives. Their personal lives and their family lives are not all messed up—they come from a base of good character. They also are usually very confident and they take the time to do what your teacher did to you—to treat you with uncommon respect and courtesy.

They also, I think, explicitly teach principles rather than practices so that rules don't take the place of human judgment. You gradually come to have faith in your own judgment in making decisions because of the affirmation of such a mentor. Good mentors care about you—you can feel the sincerity of their caring. It's like the expression, "I don't care how much you know until I know how much you care."

Wright

Most people are fascinated with the new television shows about being a survivor. What has been the greatest comeback that you've made from adversity in your career or your life?

Covey

When I was in grade school I experienced a disease in my legs. It caused me to use crutches for a while. I tried to get off them fast and get back. The disease wasn't corrected yet so I went back on crutches for another year. The disease went to the other leg and I went on for another year. It essentially took me out of my favorite thing—athletics—and it took me more into being a student. So that was kind of a life-defining experience which at the time seemed very negative, but has proven to be the basis on which I've focused my life—being more of a learner.

Wright

Principle-centered learning is basically what you do that's different from anybody I've read or listened to.

Covey

The concept is embodied in the far-eastern expression, "Give a man a fish, you feed him for the day; teach him how to fish, you feed him for a lifetime." When you teach principles that are universal and timeless, they don't belong to just any one person's religion or to a particular culture or geography. They seem to be timeless and universal like the ones we've been talking about here: trustworthiness, honesty, caring, service, growth, and development. These are universal principles. If you focus on these things then little by little people become independent of you and then they start to believe in themselves and their own judgment becomes better. You don't need as many rules. You don't need as much bureaucracy and as many controls and you can empower people.

The problem in most business operations today—and not just business but non-business—is that they're using the industrial model in an information age. Arnold Toynbee, the great historian, said, "You can pretty well summarize all of history in four words: nothing fails like success." The industrial model was based on the asset of the machine. The information model is based on the asset of the person—the knowledge worker. It's an altogether different model. But the machine model was the main asset of the twentieth century. It enabled productivity to increase fifty times. The new asset is intellectual and social capital—the qualities of people and the quality of the relationship they have with each other. Like Toynbee said, "Nothing fails like success." The industrial model does not work in an information age. It requires a focus on the new wealth, not capital and material things.

A good illustration that demonstrates how much we were into the industrial model, and still are, is to notice where people are on the balance sheet. They're not found there. Machines are found there. Machines become investments. People are on the profit and loss statement and people are expenses. Think of that—if that isn't bloodletting.

Wright

It sure is.

When you consider the choices you've made down through the years, has faith played an important role in your life?

Covey

It has played an extremely important role. I believe deeply that we should put principles at the center of our lives, but I believe that God is the source of those principles. I did not invent them. I get credit sometimes for some of the Seven Habits material and some of the other things I've done, but it's really all based on principles that have been given by God to all of His children from the beginning of time. You'll find that you can teach these same principles from the sacred texts and the wisdom literature of almost any tradition. I think the ultimate source of that is God and that is one thing you can absolutely depend upon—in God we trust.

Wright

If you could have a platform and tell our audience something you feel would help them or encourage them, what would you say?

Covey

I think I would say to put God at the center of your life and then prioritize your family. No one on their deathbed ever wished they spent more time at the office.

Wright

That's right. We have come down to the end of our program and I know you're a busy person, but I could talk with you all day Dr. Covey.

Covey

It's good to talk with you as well and to be a part of this program. It looks like an excellent one that you've got going on here.

Wright

Thank you.

We have been talking today with Dr. Stephen R. Covey, co-founder and vice-chairman of Franklin Covey Company. He's also the author of *The 7 Habits of Highly Effective People,* which has been ranked as a number one bestseller by the *New York Times*, selling more than fourteen million copies in thirty-eight languages.

Dr. Covey, thank you so much for being with us today on *Speaking of Success!*

Covey

Thank you for the honor of participating.

About The Author

Stephen R. Covey was recognized in 1996 as one of Time magazine's twenty-five most influential Americans and one of Sales and Marketing Management's top twenty-five power brokers. Dr. Covey is the author of several acclaimed books, including the international bestseller, The 7 Habits of Highly Effective People. It has sold more than fifteen million copies in thirty-eight languages throughout the world. Other bestsellers authored by Dr. Covey include First Things First, Principle-Centered Leadership (with sales exceeding one million), and The 7 Habits of Highly Effective Families.

Dr. Covey's newest book, The 8th Habit: From Effectiveness to Greatness, which was released in November 2004, rose to the top of several bestseller lists, including New York Times, Wall Street Journal, USA Today, Money, Business Week, and Amazon.com and Barnes & Noble. The 8th Habit . . . has sold more than 360,000 copies.

Dr. Covey earned his undergraduate degree from the University of Utah, his MBA from Harvard, and completed his doctorate at Brigham Young University. While at Brigham Young University, he served as assistant to the President and was also a professor of business management and organizational behavior. He received the National Fatherhood Award in 2003, which, as the father of nine and grandfather of forty-four, he says is the most meaningful award he has ever received.

Dr. Covey currently serves on the board of directors for the Points of Light Foundation. Based in Washington, D.C., the Foundation, through its partnership with the Volunteer Center National Network, engages and mobilizes millions of volunteers from all walks of life—businesses, nonprofits, faith-based organizations, low-income communities, families, youth, and older adults—to help solve serious social problems in thousands of communities.

Dr. Stephen R. Covey
www.stephencovey.com

Chapter 11

JACQUELYN FERGUSON

THE INTERVIEW

David Wright (Wright)

Today we're talking with Jacquelyn Ferguson. Jacquelyn has designed and presented programs on stress management, diversity, workplace sexual harassment, and customer service. Her mission is to inspire people to live a conscious life of personal responsibility in their relations with themselves and with others. Jackie has worked with literally hundreds of thousands of people throughout North America, the United Kingdom, Australia, and points in between. She has authored four audio programs and has a weekly published column, "Stress for Success." She is also a professional and personal development coach, helping people achieve more success with less stress.

Jackie, welcome to *Speaking of Success.*

Jacquelyn Ferguson (Ferguson)

Thanks David.

Wright

So what does success mean to you?

Ferguson

The meaning of success is so personal and each of us must define it for ourselves. To me it means several things:

- living a lifestyle that is *not* the typical rat race; I need lots of control over my schedule (in other words, not nine to five o'clock),
- working only at the work I love, which is speaking and training and writing a newspaper column,
- being surrounded by wonderful family and friends whom I love and with whom I have tons of fun,
- lots of travel and adventure,
- and of course, financial security is nice.

Wright

Let's start with the first one—a lifestyle that is *not* the typical rat race. What does that mean to you?

Ferguson

My father was a wonderful professional role model for me. Being the youngest of six kids, by the time I was growing up he had already made his business a success and was able to hire people and delegate much of his responsibilities to them. I know he worked endlessly to get his business off the ground and went above and beyond the call of duty for his customers in his younger years. By the time he was in his forties it seemed to me that his days were not terribly stressful. He had great control over how he spent his time and that appealed to me immensely.

Since I earned my undergraduate degree in 1970 I've only worked six years at the typical nine-to-five job. As much as I loved the job it drove me nuts! And even though my boss was great and gave me lots of independence and leeway, it didn't afford me enough of the control over my days that I wanted. I knew it wasn't for me and I knew I had to find something that fit me better.

I didn't consciously create my new work/home lifestyle; it just evolved.

I started my business, InterAction Associates, in 1982, and have worked out of my home ever since. I love it! I don't have to dress up or even comb my hair if I don't want to, unless I have an appointment. It would kill me to have to use a videophone some day.

My cats come to visit me and I take that as a reason to take a break. I get household chores done here and there whenever I feel like it. It's easy to fit in time for my workouts.

I realize this is not for everyone. Many people need the discipline and the social contact an office environment offers. However, not I—I'm very disciplined. By 9:00 AM at the latest every morning I'm in my office ready to start. I'm late only on the days when I've returned from a trip late the night before; then I sleep late. And that's what I mean—I want to be able to do what I want when I want.

Throughout my career I've also made sure I have lots of time off. From mid-December to mid-January, and two weeks here and two weeks there multiplied several times a year, I probably have at least three months off a year. I'm still "working" but it's at my home office researching and writing new programs, which I love to do.

Wright

It sounds like you had this vision of a lifestyle that would work for you then you made it happen.

Ferguson

Yes, I've always been pretty good at knowing what I want to accomplish and understanding and living my priorities.

My top three priorities, which over the years have all tied for first at one point or another, are family, friends, and work. Sometimes one rises to the top of the list and at other times another does.

If I were to make my career the top priority most of the time I'm sure I could make a far greater income. However, money has never particularly motivated me except for basic financial security. Neither my husband nor I is much of a materialist so we don't crave possessions as some people do. We don't want to spend our way into a corner. As my husband has always said, "You don't own your possessions; they own you"—how true, how true. We like the flexibility of not being tied to debt.

When I first started my business back in 1982, my career did take front and center. I worked very hard to get my name out there, which included doing lots and lots of free presentations for whomever. I joined lots of boards of directors and volunteered for all kinds of community projects.

Eventually my business got off the ground and I became very busy traveling around the country and the world doing workshops and speeches. It took me two years of saying "no" to requests from people in the community who were asking me to join this or do that. I can't believe it took two years before they quit calling me.

Wright

So setting limits is easy for you.

Ferguson

Setting limits is something that can be very difficult for some people, especially women. It certainly used to be difficult for me. Women are so strongly socialized to please everyone and so hesitant to do something we fear would upset anyone.

Back in the 1980s I read a book (I don't remember the name) that stated it's easier to like someone whom you respect. If you respect yourself enough to set limits so you can focus on your most important priorities, you'll teach others to also respect your limits. This author encouraged women to make decisions based on earning respect not on getting someone to like you. At that point in my life I needed to learn that. But too many of us avoid saying "no" for fear of not being liked without realizing that being all things to all people actually brings us less respect and people can end up liking us less! Go figure.

So I learned assertiveness and how to set limits and that's why it's no longer difficult for me. Some people have called me selfish for getting my needs met, but I call it knowing what I want and living my life in a way that honors that.

Another book I read, *How to Put More Time into Your Life,* by Dr. Dru Scott, taught me tons of wonderful things including the importance of focusing on the important and ignoring the trivial. This, over time, also helped me curb my perfectionism.

Dr. Scott has you answer what I now call the two magic questions: regarding your life, what do you want or need more of and what do you want or need less of? Throughout the years I continually answer these questions and the answers keep me on track. At the time I read her book I wanted fewer community commitments so I learned to set limits. I wanted more adventure and travel so I hooked up with CareerTrack Seminars that sent me throughout the world. Life is good!

Asking and answering these two questions about anything that stresses you or challenges you and then following the answers will little by little lead you where you want and need to be. It sure has worked for me. I could die happy tomorrow because I've lived a wonderful and full life—the life I wanted to live.

Wright

It seems that you've enjoyed most of what you've done in your life.

Ferguson

I must love what I do. Every job I had before I began my own business I loved. The day when I stopped loving it was the day I started planning my next move. Spending too much negative energy on something is simply not an option for me.

I just don't understand working at something year after year that a person not only doesn't love but actually dislikes or hates. The negative energy this creates must be exhausting.

Some people may stay with jobs they hate because there are no other jobs in the area in which they live. My response to that would be to either be grateful for a job of any kind where I live or I'd move somewhere where I could find a job more to my liking.

Others find themselves in a rut keeping an okay job because it gets the kids through school and pays the mortgage. I hope these people focus on their love of taking care of their children and on being grateful to have a job that affords them to do so. With this as their focus they'll have much less stress, which interestingly allows their minds to be more creative in searching for and finding other options.

Wright

Is being grateful important?

Ferguson

Absolutely! Gratefulness allows you live at a less stressed space. It encourages you to look for the good and to either downplay the negative or better, to do something about it. What do you want or need more of and less of? Ask the questions and follow the answers.

If people in a geographic area with limited professional opportunities want a better job and would have to move to get one, they will need to be able to also move out of their comfort zone. You'll never grow if you don't. If people decide to stay with their hated job then I would encourage them to remain conscious about their choice. Every time they hear themselves complain, they need to say, "I choose to keep this job" versus blaming their lot in life on outside forces.

Lots of blaming and complaining are signs of victimhood. Victims are very stressed out people because they perceive no or very few options. For victims to feel better, whomever they are blaming must change. But whoever that is—the boss, the organization for which they work, the community, etc.—are all beyond their control. A perception of not enough control is by definition stress. Their only power and control is in what they choose to do. If you don't like the results, then make different choices that are within your control to make.

Wright

It sounds like you're very big into personal responsibility.

Ferguson

You bet! Personal responsibility is almost my middle name. I've had a blessed life regarding who my parents were and how I was raised. I realize that for me to make riskier choices may be easier than for someone who had great turmoil growing up.

Even considering those who had a lot of early life challenges, there's a point at which they must take charge. Keep in mind that lots of blaming and complaining about something or someone turns you into a victim of that very person or situation. Even if people who have made some poor decisions like continuing with terrible dietary and exercise habits for the past thirty years and now are suffering physical consequences, if they choose to continue in their bad health habit ways, at least they need to remember that this is what they choose. Take responsibility. No one else is in charge of what they do to their bodies. By staying conscious of their choice, one day they are more likely to realize they could take responsibility and make healthier choices. And that's very empowering.

Wright

You seem so passionate about your work and your message of personal responsibility. How did you come upon doing the work you love?

Ferguson

By sheer accident. I was working at a mental health center as a program director when the director of the local college's "Women's Center" (remember when colleges had those?) asked me to conduct an assertiveness seminar. I said "yes" and fell in love with this work instantly.

My work over the last twenty-four years has absolutely been a labor of love. In 1980 I learned that training, speaking, and writing were my passions. I love everything about this profession! I love doing the research required to build a base of knowledge for any of the programs I present. I love writing curricula. It's a challenge with an audience of hundreds of very different people to present information in a way that virtually everybody can follow and understand my train of thought. The world of ideas is what intrigues me and isn't that what training and speaking are all about?

Ultimately the actual presentation of my programs—standing up there and delivering my message—is very exciting and motivating to me. Perhaps that explains why the only "A" grade in my entire high school career was in speech class! I was meant to do this.

My husband tells me that at my core I am a teacher. I have a passion to offer information to audiences that I think can help them with whatever the topic of the day happens to be.

My mission in all the work I do is to inspire you to live a conscious life of personal responsibility in your relations with yourself and with others. So if my presentation topic of the day is diversity, for example, my mission is to help you identify some of the stereotypes that operate in you so you can be responsible to consciously either question them and hopefully challenge them or to choose to continue judging and stereotyping people while consciously admitting that they are assumptions on your part, not necessarily facts.

Wright

It's worthy of note that you are so interested in diversity when you grew up in a small town. What kind of an impact did this have on you?

Ferguson

Yes, I grew up a small farming community in southwest Minnesota. Everyone was pretty much the same—mostly middle class, either farmers or small businesspeople who depended upon the farmers. They were primarily Scandinavians and others of northern European descent, and mostly Lutheran. I think growing up in this largely homogonous environment, along with having a mother who traveled the world via her mind through books, created in me a strong need for adventure and seeking out that which was different. She always encouraged us to be curious about the world and its people. I'm sure that's why I joined the Peace Corps in 1971. I served in Colombia from 1971 to 1973. What an adventure!

Wright

I can only imagine that an experience such as the Peace Corps must have been life altering.

Ferguson

No doubt. Throughout my high school and undergraduate years I was a very mediocre student. During high school I received multiple failing slips most quarters! I had this assumption that my older five brothers and sisters were so much more intelligent than I, so in high school especially, I just slept. It was probably my way of not competing since I assumed I'd come out on the short end of the stick. My undergraduate career was not stellar either.

But when I was in seventh grade I'll never forget seeing my first advertisement for the Peace Corps. I made a mental note and told myself I would be a Peace Corps volunteer some day. I tucked away that thought and don't remember having it again until I applied in my senior year of college.

When they accepted me a year later I was ecstatic! I was getting out into the bigger world! I could hardly wait! It also scared me to death! I knew absolutely no one and I certainly had never been outside of the United States.

But being part of the Peace Corps is not unlike having your parents take care of you. They tell you where to go, they pay for transportation and living expenses, they house you, they teach you, etc.

Serving with other mostly young people from around the country was a gift as well—so many different people and so many different ideas all coming together for a common purpose. We truly were very optimistic and idealistic and wanted desperately to help. I am still close friends with many I served with.

But we also wanted adventure! Just learning to live in a very different culture and having to speak Spanish were great experiences! Flying down the Andes Mountains in buses with bald tires that should have been retired twenty years earlier, driven by macho drivers who raced other vehicles on treacherous mountain curves was so different. And for that I loved it.

We volunteers were thrown out of our comfort zones and you either learned to sink or swim. I'm grateful I learned to swim, and swim well. It boosted my confidence incredibly! I went from seeing myself as average scholastically at best to being thrown into an environment where I was expected to do things I had no idea how to do—and I succeeded! The lessons I learned were invaluable!

Wright

Such as?

Ferguson

My first year I worked for a social service agency in Neiva called PINA. My job included working with severely malnourished children. What an eye-opener for a twenty-two-year-old from a farm state!

One day I was holding a three-year-old girl who weighed less than eighteen pounds. She was so fragile. When she'd cry you had to hold your ear next to her mouth to hear anything. One day after holding her for quite some time, I eventually put her back into her crib. Much to my horror, she died a couple of minutes later. Of course, I blamed myself. What could I have done to keep her alive? Which signals from her failing body did I miss and not report to the doctor (not that we had a doctor on site)? Do I belong here in this country? Should I go home?

After agonizing over these questions for a couple of weeks, and after almost packing my bags to return home, I learned from others' encouragement and from my own pondering of these questions that I didn't make her sick. I did the best I could to make her life comfortable. It wasn't my fault.

This experience taught me much about not taking personally things beyond my control. Later, when I became a mental health therapist, it helped me leave my work at work, unlike many in social services who carry their clients' burdens with them and who become burned out quickly.

Wright

What else did you learn from the Peace Corps experience?

Ferguson

My family was never much into materialism and my stint in the Peace Corps taught me even more how insignificant and unimportant possessions are. The people I worked with were so incredibly poor. Many families I knew lost children to malnutrition. My experiences there taught me that relationships and doing what you love are much more important than what you have.

I also learned that pursuing my dreams of travel and adventure are absolutely worth the risk. Without taking risks life can get pretty dull and repetitive. I need to shake up my brain by doing something very different quite often.

Wright

Like what?

Ferguson

Like signing up with the original CareerTrack Seminars company that moved me from presenting to local audiences to national ones and then onto international audiences—from audiences in the dozens to audiences in the hundreds. I've presented in dozens of cities worldwide from Los Angeles to London, San Antonio to Sydney, Australia and many points in between. The world is a fascinating place and I've seen a lot of it. CareerTrack took care of all of the details and I just sailed into a town for a presentation and sailed out. I'm very grateful for those years.

My husband and I also seek adventure through our vacations. Whether it's struggling through quicksand on the Caribbean island of Roatan, or traveling into the bush of Africa, we've seen and done a lot.

My approach to international travel, whether in Europe or South America, is to see the country as the average person of that country sees it. So in Europe we travel in the comfort of their great trains or rent nice cars. In South America it means risking our lives on the not so safe buses. At least in Zimbabwe the buses were safer and didn't pick up passengers on the road if they had no open seats.

We have also gotten a lot of adventure and excitement through skiing. There's nothing like flying down a mountain run (probably faster than I should since I'm not a refined skier but more of a bulldog) with the wind in my ears and the exhilaration of reaching the bottom in one piece.

Another adventure my husband and I embarked upon was a one-year, motorhome trip around the United States into Western Canada and up to Alaska and back. What an adventure again! This is such a beautiful country, as is Canada. That trip didn't satisfy our need to travel as much as it showed us which areas we want to return to and new areas we want to cover.

This trip came at an important point for us both. My husband had been burned out from his work, as had I. And my mother and father became ill at the end of their lives at the same time. After one and a half years of care-giving on top of the career burnout already brewing, we both needed a serious break.

Our year-long sabbatical was certainly an expensive choice; but it was definitely worth it for our well-being. Before we left on our trip we were both starting to show signs of burnout, both physical and emotional. After a year on the road we returned full of physical and mental health and energy, ready to hit the road running. Again, the risk proved worth it.

Wright

You stated earlier than financial health was important to your definition of success and yet you took off an entire year.

Ferguson

Financial security is important to both my husband and me and must include, and indeed it requires, living within our means. Because we haven't carried credit card debt since 1986 and we pay cash for our cars (not new ones) our only debt since 1986 has been our mortgage.

Plus we made investments in real estate in southwest Florida that turned out to be nicely profitable. The money we spent on the sabbatical did not come out of our retirement funds and our burnout was so significant that we decided it was worth the money and the risk.

Living within our means has allowed us to make choices that we otherwise could not make. So I guess this means that another component of success for me is the freedom from financial burden, which allows us to change on a dime when it seems like the right thing to do.

Wright

There's that risk thing again.

Ferguson

We don't take foolish risks. I'm the numbers cruncher for our household and I'll look at things from ninety-two perspectives before jumping. So far the choices we've made have been good ones so it gives us the confidence to continue taking calculated risks when we think it's time.

Wright

Of what you mentioned at the very beginning that was important to you for your own definition of success, which is the most important to you?

Ferguson

The most important element of success to me is living a life that's full of love in my marriage and with my family and friends. I've been married for almost twenty-eight years. My husband is my one and only. We are and always have been on the same path in life and are best friends. For example, neither of us has been willing to be workaholics and have always made work/home balance a priority.

We are a great team. He makes me laugh. Throughout the decades he introduced me to skiing, motorcycle riding, and spending lots of money on great stereo equipment. I've introduced him to international travel and a greater appreciation of different cultures of the world and classical music.

For over twenty years I've also been surrounded by a large circle of women friends, along with their husbands and kids, without whom I'm sure I'd have gone nuts on occasion over the decades. There are a dozen of us and each woman is so different, affording all of us a variety of personalities, strengths, and support one could ever hope for. I believe in the research that says those who have lots of loving people in their lives are healthier and probably live longer. We laugh so hard so frequently that it just carries the stress of the world away.

Wright

Jackie, in all of what you've said, you've never mentioned a mentor or role model. Who influenced you the most?

Ferguson

My parents were my original motivators. They were very good at encouraging without pushing; letting me decide what I wanted versus what they wanted me to do. My father wasn't wild about my going into the Peace Corps but only mentioned it briefly a couple of times then backed off. They taught us that we could do anything we wanted that we were willing to put our minds into.

They both had a great deal of integrity as well. My father used to say, "There's nothing worse than a liar." To this day, I cannot lie. The truth is virtually always the better way to go and doesn't require negative energy. They did what they said they'd do and so do I; so do all of my siblings as well.

All throughout my public school career we had a music director, Mr. Opland, who was an absolute perfectionist and had expectations that were also perfectionistic. When I talk to former classmates, so many of them say that he was a huge influence on them. He showed us through his expectations of us that we could perform better than any of us would have thought possible. Our musical groups, both vocal and instrumental, were perennial winners in all local, state, and even national competitions.

However, I have had only one true mentor in my entire professional life—my graduate school advisor, Dr. Keith LeVake. With my mediocre scholastic background I didn't feel totally comfortable entering grad school. Then I discovered that my advisor was the one whom other students described as a tyrant and ogre. Great!

But he wasn't that at all. He was blunt and sometimes brutally honest. He expected a lot of me as well as of others. He also saw something in me that I had seen only glimpses of now and again. Soon after classes started he decided I was going to be his star student. He gave me one challenge after another. He raised the bar higher and higher, and by golly if I didn't meet the challenge each and every time! Plus he gave me the best graduate assistantship. Graduate school was a huge success for me, and with Keith's help I developed much more self-confidence. I'll always be grateful to him.

Otherwise, professionally, I haven't had anyone pave the way for me. I think that's a far more common occurrence for men. Hopefully the younger generations are better at mentoring their female as well as their male employees.

My husband has been hugely influential in my career too. He's incredibly supportive and happens to be great with words. So when I'm trying to write a story or develop examples for whatever presentation, he'll often help me. He gets immediately to the point and usually with great humor.

Wright

Finally, Jackie, what is your message to readers so they can learn from your success?

Ferguson

It certainly has to begin with knowing what would define the success that would make you happy. If you don't have a vision of what that means, how can you create it?

Your vision also has to be true to yourself. This requires that you listen to yourself and acknowledge when something is wrong for you. Believe me, between your thoughts, emotions, and your body, the message is being sent. You just have to listen and act accordingly. Move toward what gives you joy and happiness and away from what pulls you down.

Once you let your truth emerge and stop fighting it, it's amazing how the world opens up possibilities to you.

If you haven't figured out what that vision is, there are great creative techniques to help you search for your own truth. I fully believe that each and every person knows, at some level of awareness, what to do to live a better life. The trick is to quiet yourself regularly, ask good questions (including the "what you want/need more of and less of"), and listen for your answers. Little by little, if you follow your own advice, you'll end up where you want to be.

Then you certainly must have the confidence and willingness to take risks to make the dream a reality. If you need to enhance your confidence, take small steps. It's a much easier way to stretch your comfort zone a little at a time. There's nothing wrong with that strategy.

I remember research done in the 1990s at the University of Arizona, I believe, which asked retirees what their top regrets were. They listed not taking enough risks and not being more assertive. This makes so much sense to me.

Since I've always been a risk-taker I realize it is easier for me than it might be for someone who hasn't taken very many. But I had no real experience at risk-taking when I took my first really big one joining the Peace Corps and going to a foreign country not knowing a soul. That taught me that taking a risk is a good thing.

And you need to be assertive to pursue your vision. Don't confuse assertiveness with aggressiveness. Being assertive means you stand up for yourself in a way that is respectful of the rights of others. When your rights and those of another collide, if you are an assertive person you are willing to negotiate in a way that recognizes that everyone's needs are as important to them as yours are to you.

If your vision requires that you make significant changes, others around you may not be too excited and supportive of these changes. I mentioned earlier after starting my business that it took me a couple of years of assertively setting limits with people from the community when I was asked to volunteer for something. This required that I not let anyone deter me, like the one time when I heard that someone had said less-than-great things about me when I turned down his request. You have to be willing to stand up for what you want.

Hard work is also required to create your vision. Wasn't it Jack Canfield who said, "Where your energy goes, results show"? If you work hard (and smart) you'll get the results you want. On the other hand, if you just day-dream about what you want but do nothing substantial to make it happen, then your result will be great day-dreams. If you want a different life, or different parts of your life, you'll need to have the vision and *do* whatever is required to make it happen.

Finally, as a stress management expert, I can't say often enough how important self-care and balance are to success.

Life balance changes throughout your lifetime, requiring ongoing assessment of your satisfaction with it. For instance, a few years ago I felt like I needed more spirituality. Two opportunities seemed appealing: I rejoined our local symphony chorus and once again am singing the music I was raised on. It fills me with joy. The other was to become a "cuddler" at the local hospital. One night a week I volunteer and work with premature babies, changing their diapers, feeding, and rocking them. To me it's the sweetest volunteer job in the world.

Being in a state of balance is just a dream to too many Americans. Our work situation certainly doesn't help. We work twelve and a half weeks a year more than the Germans! Think about it! Three months more a year! This is nuts and once caught up in it—making more money, spending more money—you find yourself with high cholesterol, high blood pressure, a bad back, and who knows what else! There are more things in this world than racing around working and mindlessly doing what you did yesterday. "Quiet Mind Journaling" is a technique I teach to help people figure out how they want their lives to be and how to get out of the rut of the American (crazy) lifestyle.

Too many Americans, however, work so incredibly hard, putting in sixty or more hours a week, month after month, even year after year. At some point, their bodies (if not their families) will present them with a bill.

I teach a lot of self-care to help people who are caught up in the runaway American lifestyle that will help pull them back from I call their *Stress Cliff.* This is where stress begins to damage you physically, mentally, and emotionally. By slowing it down a little here and a little there you'll limit the damages of stress and give yourself more energy to do the very things you're doing.

The best antidote to a too-stressful life is to figure out what's most important to you and arrange your life so you can live your priorities. All else falls into place when you find the peace of mind that you are doing what you are meant to do.

About the Author

For over twenty years, Jacquelyn Ferguson has designed and presented programs on stress management, diversity, workplace/sexual harassment, and customer service.

Jackie has worked with literally hundreds of thousands of people throughout North America, the United Kingdom, Australia, and points in between. She has authored four audio programs and has a weekly, published column, "Stress for Success."

Look for her next book, *Slow Down, You Move Too Fast: Get Into Stress Shape,* later this year.

She's also a Professional and Personal Development Coach helping people achieve more success with less stress.

Jacquelyn Ferguson
InterAction Associates
4596 Little River Lane
Ft. Myers, FL 33905
Phone: 239.693.8111
E-mail: jferg8@aol.com
www.jackieferguson.com

Chapter 12

BOB YOUNGLOVE

THE INTERVIEW

David Wright (Wright)

Today we're talking with Bob Younglove. Bob is a graduate instructor at Johns Hopkins University, Vice President of the National Association for Self-Esteem, a member of the Board of Directors of the Maryland Center for Character Education, and a speaker for the Achievement Counts Program for High School Students. His passion is to help parents, teachers, and coaches sharpen their skills at positively influencing children and teens to believe in their talent and ability for success.

Bob, welcome to *Speaking of Success.*

Success means different things to different people. What does success mean to you?

Bob Younglove (Younglove)

Success is making progress on a joyful journey, day by day, moving you toward your vision of your ideal life. It requires making a commitment to do at least one itty-bitty task each day to move you toward your dreams. It is feeling successful every day because you will know that when you put your head down on your pillow at night, you will have taken at least some action toward the achievement of your goals.

Wright

So you see success as a daily habit, not a final destination. How does one stay focused and motivated to put consistent effort toward goal achievement?

Younglove

I believe in the psychological principle that *we move toward what we picture and* we *become like the person we picture ourselves to be.* When we have an inspiring and compelling vision of how we want to be living in the future, we are pulled toward that picture. If we picture ourselves to be healthy, full of energy, and highly productive, then our brain actually goes to work searching for opportunities that will take us in the direction of our dreams.

However, when we do not move beyond picturing what we have right now, we will likely get more of the same. It is natural to think of the way things are and all the things we have to do today, and not think about how we want things to be better. For many people, tomorrow will be a repeat of today, this month will look like last month, and next year might be much like this year. Now that's okay, if you presently have everything you want in your life. *However,* if you have dreams and wishes for something better—good health, joyful relationships, a new career, etc.—then creating that picture and taking positive actions toward that vision are essential elements of success.

If we spend all of our time and energy just to maintain what we currently have, life may be very frustrating. I call that "treading water." It takes lots of energy just to stay afloat and it is exhausting, yet we aren't going anywhere. At the end of the day we haul ourselves out of the swimming pool of life only to find we haven't moved forward.

I recommend swimming instead of treading water. Swimming takes less energy and it moves us toward an appealing destination. But swimming rather than treading water requires that we change our stroke—our daily actions. It also requires recognizing we have a larger pool of opportunities and holding the belief that we can learn to swim.

Wright

As a Performance Coach, how do you help people recognize opportunities and change behaviors to start to swim?

Younglove

It starts with having a vision of how we want our life to be different—better—in the future. A destination to swim toward is very appealing. I ask all my clients to create their Fantasy of an Ideal Day—the way they would like a typical day to be in three to five years. It is a fantasy in that you don't have to worry about how to make it happen or if it is realistic or possible. The fantasy vision points a direction and provides motivation. If you can daydream, then you can create a wonderful vision of your future—where you are living, how you are living, how you look and feel, the quality of your relationships, how you spend your time and use your talent, what you do for fun, etc. It's all very exciting to have this to look forward to.

Wright

That sounds great, but how do you get people started on the process of taking the actions that will make the fantasy a reality?

Younglove

I mentioned that we need to change what we do—we need to move from treading water to swimming. That means examining how we need to change our daily behaviors. What new habits and characteristics do we need to develop to lead us to our goals? We need to recognize that if we keep doing what we have always done, we will keep getting what we have always gotten.

I believe that most of us already know what we need to do to be healthier, happier, and more successful. We just don't do it. Success is turning our good intentions into positive results. The majority of my work is teaching people how to create new habits or behaviors at the subconscious level that will create greater success.

Wright

How can you create behaviors subconsciously?

Younglove

Well, it starts with conscious thoughts and small actions, repeated until the behavior becomes a habit. Then it moves quite naturally into the subconscious. It's amazing how many things we do subconsciously! Just like learning to walk or drive a car took lots of conscious energy and practice in the beginning, we now do those complex behaviors with little or no conscious thought. The required behaviors have become part of our subconscious "autopilot."

Let me give you an example. Have you ever been driving your car home from work and realized you haven't been thinking about driving? Your conscious mind has been thinking or daydreaming about other things. Suddenly you realize that you can't remember if the traffic light at a particular intersection was red or green. In fact, you don't even remember going through that intersection. So who is really driving the car? Your subconscious mind has learned to take the data your eyes see—the traffic light changing from green to red—analyze it, and send a message to the muscles in your leg to take your foot off the accelerator and put in on the break. If it is like you to stop at red lights automatically, then the job of the subconscious self-image is to keep you acting in accordance with that expectation.

Our marvelous mind allows us to program many behaviors into habits that we do automatically.

Wright

Do you encounter people who believe they can't change who they are or how they act?

Younglove

Of course I do. Most of us have grown up with habits we believe we inherited from Aunt Agnes or Grandfather George. For example, it was easier for me to believe I was born a procrastinator than accept responsibility for choosing my habits and characteristics. Fortunately, my grandmother taught me that, "There are only two things in life you have to do: die and pay taxes. Everything else is a choice." With this insight, I learned that I could make choices about my behavior. Instead of being a life-long procrastinator, I chose to be a do-it-now person, who does what needs to be done when it needs to be done, whether I like it or not.

It all started with changing the way I thought about myself—my self-image and resulting self-expectations. We can all choose what we think, how we feel, and how we act. Think how powerful it would be to change our thinking from "I can't lose weight" or "I can't control my temper" to "I have great willpower and I will succeed at whatever I set my mind to."

Wright

That is quite a leap of faith to change what you believe to be true about yourself. How do you help someone develop that kind of confidence to be successful?

Younglove

It is a leap of faith and it is quite doable. It helps to consider that some of our beliefs about our abilities were formed in error because of early childhood experiences. For example, I can still remember the embarrassment I felt in the fifth grade when the music teacher said, "Bobby, just mouth the words." I thought, "I must sound terrible." And so I began to think and believe that I can't sing! I don't have any musical talent. As long as I held that belief, it kept me from developing my musical talent. When I chose to change my belief, I was able, with some coaching, to sing on stage in front of an audience.

Maybe you were told you can't draw, or you're clumsy, forgetful, or have Attention Deficit Disorder. If you believe that, your subconscious mind works to keep you acting in accordance with that belief. What might happen if you changed your limiting beliefs?

I start by helping people identify the qualities, characteristics, and habits that will cause them to be more successful in achieving their goals. Thanks to Stephen Covey, we have learned about the habits of highly effective people. Think of your own vision of success, for example. Would it be helpful to have the characteristic of creativity, the quality of patient persistence, or the habit of diplomatic confrontation?

Thanks to my work with teachers like Lou Tice and Jack Canfield, I have learned the strategies and techniques for creating a new self-image that facilitates these new behaviors at a primarily subconscious level. Since we feed the subconscious mind with messages from our conscious self-talk we can reprogram our self-image and its autopilot function by consciously changing our self-talk.

I prefer to use Focus Cards at least twice a day, seven days a week, to shape desired beliefs and behaviors. My Focus Card has four parts, written on a three- by five-inch card. The first part lists the quality I desire. Let's say I want to be "sensitive, patient, and understanding in dealing with my children." Second, I list all the reasons why having that behavior is important to me, such as wanting my children to feel that they can come and talk with me about absolutely anything, knowing that I will listen, try to understand, and help them consider the options. The third part is a sentence or two that describes me acting with the quality I desire. I want this sentence to create a vivid picture in my mind of what I look like, act like, and sound like when patiently dealing with my children, regardless of the situation.

What is unique about my approach is step four. On the back of the three- by five-inch card, I list all the little things I need to do to achieve my goal. For example, I need to remain calm, speak softly, and not interrupt my children. To do this, I need to take a deep breath, and say, "Remember, I love you very much." I need to say, "Help me understand" rather than ask the dreaded, "Why did you do that?" When I can picture myself consistently doing all these little behaviors, then I have re-programmed the expectation of my behavior and I will begin to automatically act that way.

Wright

You are saying that people can change their typical behaviors to ones more productive in meeting their goals. How long does this re-programming process take? How many habits can be reprogrammed at one time?

Younglove

I can show people many ways in which they allow their autopilot to control their behaviors. We already use this marvelous feature of our mind to allow us to use a computer keyboard, play a musical instrument, or drive a car. Once we have learned keyboard skills, we don't have to consciously think where each letter is, we just think the word and the subconscious brain tells our fingers to move to the right letters. What most of us don't appreciate, however, is that we can control the programming of our autopilot to lead us to greater success.

Sometimes we create a program of belief that limits our ability. When we say, "I can't remember names," we are actually giving an instruction to our memory to not remember names. The fact that we can recall the name later tells us that we had the information all along, but did not expect to recall it in a timely manner. I suggest we consciously program a more positive message to our subconscious mind: "I have a great memory and the information I want to recall will soon come to me." Then stop trying so hard to remember and just let it pop into your mind in the next few minutes.

To answer your question about how long it takes to reprogram an old habit, it depends on how strong the old belief is. Some research suggests that it may take four to six weeks to reprogram the subconscious mind. I grew up being shy and avoiding conflict, so it took a while before I could begin to picture myself being confident and diplomatically assertive in asking for what I wanted. That is why the little behaviors on the back of my Focus Card were so important in gradually moving me toward my goal. Success in demonstrating each of the little, itty-bitty behaviors on my card built my confidence and caused me to believe that I could achieve my larger goal.

I have probably worked on well over a hundred behavior changes in the last twenty-five years. But I work on no more than six at a time. I guess you could work on many changes at one time, provided you were dedicated to putting forth the time and consistent effort. I have found it takes me about a minute or two to read each of my Focus Cards, close my eyes, picture the new behavior, and allow myself to savor how good it feels to be acting in a successful way. That means that it takes me about ten minutes each morning when I wake up and ten minutes each evening before I go to sleep. That doesn't sound like much—until I am in a rush to get somewhere or very tired at night. The consistent effort of reading the Focus Card twice a day, every day is needed to achieve success.

Wright

How do you know if and when someone is really ready to make this kind of change?

Younglove

That's an important question in my line of work. "Is the person ready now to be coached?" Unless the client is really ready, there is no sense trying to lose weight, quit smoking, or try to overcome shyness. "Trying" implies doubt about your ability to be successful. You will generally try and then give up as soon as it gets difficult. When that happens, you will feel like a failure and you may believe you just don't have the willpower to succeed. Unless you are really ready to do it, you are better off not "trying."

I use a little formula to determine readiness for change:

1. What is your level of dissatisfaction with the present situation? If you are in your comfort zone, even if you are miserably comfortable, you will resist change. When you are fed up with your life, then you're ready. But "don't jump out of the frying pan into the fire." Changing just to get away from a

bad situation may put you in a worse spot; for example, quitting your job before you have another one lined up.

2. Do you know in what way you want to be different? Do you have a compelling vision of how you want your life to be in the future? Can you picture it? Do you know what your options are?
3. Do you have the knowledge and know-how to start moving toward your vision? Are you aware of all the ways to get what you want? Do you know who to ask for help? Do you have any ideas about where to get the information you need? Do you have a plan of action?
4. Most importantly, what is the extent of your self-confidence? Do you believe in yourself and your ability to be successful? Do you trust and believe that when you make up your mind to do something, you will do it?

By calculating the scores in each area, I can determine a person's readiness for change and more importantly, I can suggest ways the person can increase his or her readiness for success. Timing has a lot to do with success. The first thing to do is to get yourself mentally and emotionally ready to succeed.

Wright

Bob, tell me how you have used this approach to creating success in your own career.

Younglove

I would be delighted to. First, I chose my career based on what I love to do—help others. I became a juvenile counselor because I love working with teenagers. I have also chosen to teach at Johns Hopkins University where I help college students learn effective people management skills like coaching and negotiation. Ever since I completed my service to my country as a Naval Air Controller, I have been fortunate to do the work I love.

When I was about to lose my job with the Juvenile Services Administration due to downsizing, I attended a workshop led by the late Herb Shepherd. He asked me to create a vision of an ideal day the way I wanted it to be in my future. I did, and I fell in love with my vision—having my own business, traveling the world at someone else's expense, teaching, coaching, and consulting.

The mission of my company, PATH Associates, is to help as many people as possible learn to take responsible actions in their lives to be healthier, happier, and more successful in achieving their goals. I have been fortunate to facilitate training programs on performance improvement strategies for many companies and government organizations. I have had the opportunity to help many teenagers transition through the stressful adolescent years into productive adulthood. This has been my success: for over thirty years, I have helped others have more joyful and rewarding lives.

Now, as Vice President of the National Association for Self-Esteem, and Director of its Youth Character and Confidence Initiative, I speak to parents, teachers, youth leaders, and coaches about the awesome responsibility of equipping our young people to successfully deal with life's many challenges. We can't always be right there to help children make good decisions or have the courage to face adversity, so we must help them develop the characteristics and the confidence to deal effectively with whatever happens in life.

Wright

What do you think are the biggest obstacles to people achieving success?

Younglove

One barrier to success is not determining what success means to you in every area of your life. We tend to accept others' definitions of success, or compare our achievements, status, and lifestyle to that of others. You can always find someone else's situation so good that it will make you feel like a failure.

I always tell the young athletes I coach that they are only in competition with themselves, no one else. Winning is improving on your own personal best performance, getting consistently better at what you choose to do with your talent.

Another barrier is internal and perhaps unconscious resistance that sabotages our thinking. This resistance may take the form of assumptions we make about ourselves or the things we want. The strategy is to flush out those limiting beliefs and replace them with enabling beliefs.

For example, when I started my own business I worked very hard, but, as Jack Canfield would say, I was driving with the brakes on. With the help of a friend, I uncovered a belief I didn't even realize I held. I believed that "if you were very successful in your own business it would ruin your marriage." I may have learned this from my father telling me stories of entrepreneurs who ended up in divorce court. My father may not have even intended to teach that lesson, but as children we listen and form our own conclusions. Anyway, once I realized I held that thought, I re-scripted it to be, "The more successful I am in my business, the better my relationship will be with my family." And since we move toward what we picture, that became my new reality.

Most of all, the barrier to success is taking the path of least resistance—staying in your comfort zone and blaming others for not achieving your dreams. If your current circumstances don't lend themselves to enabling your success, then you need to define the *conditions under which you are both willing and able to be successful.*

Make a list of what needs to change in your life and what the options are for making those changes. This strategy has been used by many companies to coach employees in identifying the conditions for performance improvement. Once the conditions have been identified, the challenge is to take responsibility for negotiating with others for the support, resources, and time you need to increase your success.

As an example, let me explain how I coached my youngest daughter toward success. She grew up wanting to be a nurse. However, at one point early in high school she brought home a report card that averaged out to a 1.7 with C's and D's. That wasn't going to do it for getting into college.

First I tried to motivate her to do her homework and study for tests by using rewards: cash for A's, driving privileges, etc. When that didn't work I tried taking away privileges, which she saw as punishments. That caused both a morale problem and no improvement in her performance. Finally, I told her that I knew she could get A's and B's under the right conditions. So I asked her to make a list of what would need to change—at school, at home, and with her—in order for her to be willing and able to get better grades.

After five days, she came back to me with a list of fourteen items. We sat down together and prioritized her list and then started discussing how we could best create these conditions. Together my daughter and I negotiated with the school, worked with the teachers, and made some changes at home. The result was that my daughter's grades went from a 1.7 to a 3.7. She not only graduated and went on to college, she also received a scholarship for nursing. Now she is a very successful Nurse Practitioner.

I call that a parenting success and she claims it all happened when I stopped being a boss and started being a coach. As I see it, the job of a coach is to help the person define success and then create the conditions to make it happen.

Wright

Bob, this has been most interesting. Do you have a final suggestion for readers who are striving to be successful?

Younglove

Don't go it alone! Most successful people have coaches, mentors, and guides to help show them the way and encourage them.

In my book, *SPONSOR SUCCESS: A Workbook for Turning Good Intentions Into Positive Results*, I discuss how to find the right person to be your sponsor/coach. This is usually not a best friend, but someone you look up to and respect, who will not accept your lame excuses for non-action. While we are not very good at keeping promises to ourselves, most of us are good at keeping promises to others.

A sponsor/coach can assist you in overcoming barriers, suggest new options, and most importantly, encourage you when the going gets tough. That is why we are more successful when we have a support group and a plan of action to follow. Besides, it is more fun to travel the path to success with someone you can share your challenges and achievements with. Personally, I have found it most helpful to have a "running mate" who is working on similar goals as mine because we work to help each other.

My wish for all of those who read this book is that you will honestly be able to say a year from now, "I am healthier, happier, and more successful in achieving my goals because of the way I am choosing to use my talent, my energy, and my marvelous mind."

About the Author

BOB YOUNGLOVE inspires and entertains audiences with his humorous stories and practical strategies for building character and confidence for success. Bob has combined his education in Behavioral Psychology with more than thirty years of experience as a Performance Coach, Corporate Trainer, and Change Consultant, helping people change their habits and lifestyle to be healthier, happier, and more successful. As a shy child with learning disabilities who failed the sixth grade, Bob struggled to believe in his dream for success. With the coaching support of many successful people, Bob has created and managed PATH Associates for more than thirty years. He received the ASTD Touch Award for contributions in turning classroom training into performance improvement on the job. He has facilitated the change process in numerous organizations and demonstrated how supervisors can become coaches for improved performance. He is the author of several books, including *SPONSOR SUCCESS: A Workbook for Turning Good Intentions Into Positive Results.* He is a frequent speaker on performance improvement strategies.

Bob Younglove, Performance Coach
PATH Associates
19 Coldwater Court
Towson, MD 21204
Phone: 410.821.0538
E-mail: PATHassoc@aol.com
www.PATHassociatesonline.com

Chapter 13

PATRICK WILLIAMS

THE INTERVIEW

David Wright (Wright)

Today we're talking with Dr. Patrick Williams, one of the early pioneers of coaching. Pat is often called the "Ambassador of Life Coaching." He has been a licensed psychologist since 1980 and began executive coaching in 1990 with Hewlett Packard, IBM, Kodak, and other companies along the Front Range of Colorado. He is a member of Phi Beta Kappa and a cum laude graduate of Kansas University in 1972. Pat went on to get his master's in Humanistic Psychology from the University of West Georgia in 1975 and his doctorate in Transpersonal Psychology in 1977 from the University of Northern Colorado.

Pat joined Coach U in 1996, closed his therapy practice six months later, and became a full-time coach. He was a senior trainer with Coach U from 1997–1998, when he started his own coach training school for therapists only, the Institute for Life Coach Training. He has trained over 1,700 helping professionals at the Institute for Life Coach Training and has now opened offices in Korea, Hong Kong, Istanbul, Italy, Australia, and South Africa.

Pat is the department chair of the coaching psychology program at the International University of Professional Studies (www.iups.edu) and has taught graduate coaching classes at Colorado State University and Denver University and New England Educational Institute. He is also a curriculum consultant for the Coaching Certificate program at Fielding International University (www.fielding.edu/hod/ce/ebc/faculty).

Pat is a former member of the ICF Board of Directors and co-chaired the Regulatory Committee as well. He is passionate about the profession of coaching and ensuring that it remains a respected profession.

In May of 2006, Pat was honored as the first Global Visionary Fellow by the Foundation of Coaching for his Coaching the Global Village initiative of bringing coaching methodologies to third world/developing villages.

He is the co-author of *Therapist as Life Coach: Transforming Your Practice;* Total *Life Coaching: 50+ Life Lessons, Skills, and Techniques to Enhance your Practice and Your Life;* and *Law* and *Ethics of Coaching: How to Solve and Avoid Difficult Problems in Your Practice.*

His newest book is *Becoming a Professional Life Coach: Lessons from the Institute for Life Coach Training* (Norton Professional books, March 2007).

Dr. Williams, welcome to *Speaking of Success.*

Dr. Patrick Williams (Williams)

Thank you, I'm glad to be here!

Wright

Why are you often called the "Ambassador of Life Coaching"?

Williams

Several colleagues put that moniker on me a few years ago because I do travel the world speaking about coaching and all things coaching and purposeful living—living beyond mediocrity, coaching, training, etc. I guess I'm so enthusiastic about it that people feel I'm the ambassador for the profession more than I am just for my business. That's really true—I have a passion for what coaching can do for individuals and cultures and communities because it's a shift in the way people think and communicate. I must say though that if I'm the ambassador, I wish I could get an embassy somewhere in the Caribbean Islands!

Wright

So how do you define Life Coaching?

Williams

I'll give you the short definition. In very simple language it's really a whole person, client-centered approach to someone developing a future more than getting over his or her past. What I mean by that is psycho-therapy and counseling has been there for people to get help with overcoming very difficult situations from the past or things that are causing them to be stuck in a serious way in life. Coaching is for people ready for change in their life or business.

Life Coaching is there for people who are relatively healthy and ready to design the future that they want, whether it's next week or next year or five years from now, and it's a co-creative process. When I say "whole person, client-centered co-creative," what I mean is that the coach is not the expert on anything other than coaching. I'm not the expert on my clients' lives, I'm not the expert on my clients' desires, but I will help bring out their best thinking and things they've never said before and not thought before. I have them speak it publicly, at least in conversations with their coach. It's a process of personal empowerment. Even if I, as the coach, have expertise or knowledge in an area where clients seek improvement, my primary responsibility is to coach them to their solutions, not to advise them or give them the answer based on my expertise. Coaches may share ideas and knowledge when appropriate, but it is only offered to the client as one possibility, not the only possibility. I may have some expertise, but I am not an expert on their unique life.

Wright

So how did you become a highly sought-after Life Coach?

Williams

I think in my years of being a psychologist since 1990 (you can read in my bio that my graduate degrees were in Humanistic and Transpersonal Psychology) that background lends itself more to a passion and involvement in human potential than it does in looking at human pathology, which is what clinical psychology traditionally does. I was very coach-like as a therapist. I was very enthusiastic, very positive. I would reframe people's difficult situations into what could be and before I even heard of the word "coaching" that's how I functioned as a counselor and a therapist.

In 1990 a woman came to me in Fort Collins, Colorado (where I lived for 31 years), who had a group called The People Business. She was doing a lot of executive "boot camps" where high level managers and leaders would come to get away on weekends to learn how to become more effective in their jobs. She hired me to be the coach for the highest level executives prior to the training as well as after the training because she realized that coaching is what helps things get implemented.

You probably know that people pay a lot of money to attend Stephen Covey weekends or Tony Robbins weekends or Deepak Chopra training. What happens three months later after that training? In most cases the books and the tapes are usually still sitting on the shelf and nothing has been implemented. Coaching is what makes results become sustainable over time.

As I began doing executive coaching with high level managers, I then saw the power of coaching expand in the mid-90s to the individual businessperson, small business entrepreneur, and people who just wanted to have the benefit of a coach to help them live the best life possible.

I trained with some of the best coach training organizations out there before I started my own. I hired some of the best coaches, and I've written not only the four books you mentioned, but several articles and I speak around the world. Because of that I think my reputation has developed and now I'm considered as one of the twenty-five most influential people in the field of coaching, as stated in a recent historical article on the profession of coaching.

Wright

Would you explain a little more about what you call "purposeful living"?

Williams

Absolutely. I think my job in life is to help other people live more purposely. I have a strong belief that we all have a unique individual purpose. Every human being is as unique as a snowflake or a fingerprint—there is not another person like you.

I do believe that we have some path to discover along our journey in this life. We don't often know what that is, but we do know what it's not. If you are doing something that doesn't make you happy, what would you rather be doing? That doesn't mean that everybody can have a job that is the most ideal job in the world. Maybe your job is just a job that pays the bills; but what do you do that really gives you joy or really brings you ecstasy and a sense of connection and significance?

Living purposely is living beyond mediocrity and not settling for average or just okay—to "go for the gold," to put it in Olympic language. Go for the best, and live a life that has meaning and leaves a legacy and impacts the lives of those who are living here now and will come after you. So to deliberately be "on purpose" is what I am talking about. This time in our evolution is the age of purpose.

Wright

How has coaching changed your life?

Williams

I think you can hear the enthusiasm in my voice in this interview. The profession of coaching has changed my life. I was really burning out as a therapist. I have nothing against the profession of psychology—we need very good therapists, we need good clinicians for treating the mental illnesses that people might develop. But I had done that for fifteen years and I frankly had had enough.

Seeing clients wasn't what was burning me out; what was burning me out was the health care system in America and how difficult it was to be in a profession worrying about legal concerns and payment concerns and health insurance; but I won't go into all those details. Let's just say that for me, *managed care* in the mental health field became more like *mangled care.* The system of insurance and treatment planning became way too complicated and unfair.

Coaching changed my life because it allowed me to live where I wanted to live and coach with people all over the world because most coaching is done over the telephone. It has really excited me because I'm able to work with people who pretty much already have good lives but they want to have *great* lives!

The other way coaching has impacted me is that I've become a speaker and a writer in a field I'm passionate about. I never did that as a therapist. To write about deeply academic, clinical topics was not something that I wanted to do. Coaching helped me to connect with clients and colleagues around the world and work with people who are healthy but who want to express their magnificance.

The coaching I have received from some of the best coaches in the world has inspired me to live a very happy life.

Wright

I had heard years and years ago that if you're walking down a road and see a turtle sitting on top of a fencepost, you can bet that he didn't get up there by himself! Who are the important figures, past and present, who have influenced your life's journey?

Williams

That's an interesting question. This is going to sound to your readers like an odd answer, but I'll give you the three names that always come to mind in history of those who have influenced me. It's an interesting mix.

Number one is my father. I was fortunate enough to have a father who was my best friend. He was also my early coach in sports. He was my baseball coach and basketball coach, but he was also my life coach. He never would have called himself that, but my dad was a good model of how to live with values, humor, credibility, and friendship. I owe a lot to him and the character that he instilled in me.

The second influential person was Carl Jung. He was a psychiatrist who was in Sigmund Freud's inner circle back in the turn of the previous century. Soon thereafter he broke away because Carl Jung had a more teleological or future-oriented approach to living. He felt that we are drawn to our future by living life more purposely. Freud and some of the others felt that people are trapped by their neuroses and difficulties. Jung got into the whole mind/body/spirit connection. He studied tribal cultures around the world. He researched and wrote about what drove people to live powerful lives instead of what drove people to be mentally constricted. So Carl Jung was a friend of mine—I'm sorry, not a friend of mine—a mentor of mine. (It's funny that I said "a friend of mine" because even though he was dead he did seem like a friend of mine. I'd read most of his works, I'd listened to tapes, and had studied his work, so even though Carl Jung was not alive he was an impressionable part of my life!)

The third name (and this is going to be somewhat incongruent but let me explain it) is Paul McCartney of the Beatles. I grew up in the '60s and I had every Beatles album that was ever made. I got to see them live in Colorado in 1964—I have seen two Paul McCartney concerts since then—and it's not so much the music as it is the man. What I was always impressed with about Paul is that through all the trials and tribulations of the notoriety of the Beatles and through his recent difficulties with his marriage, I really respect who he is as a person and the way he is able to avoid negative media attention and how he protects his children. Also admirable is the fact that he gives a lot of money away and doesn't seek to be on the cover of *People* magazine because of that. The lyrics of his music have always been positive and endearing.

As incongruent as it may sound, those three men: my dad, Carl Jung, and Paul McCartney have influenced me a lot in the way that I am in the world.

Wright

Over the past five or six years I have asked that question of literally hundreds if not thousands of people, and very few have mentioned their father. They always mention their mother. Do you find that?

Williams

I would find that to be true. I have a great mother too. I used to laugh in college because when I went to graduate school in psychology people wondered why I was there because I'd had a happy childhood. I was embarrassed for having a happy childhood. I didn't mean that it was perfect, so why *did* I become a psychologist and a coach? I feel it's my obligation and my life purpose to take my strengths of what I learned in a happy childhood and bring it to other people. I know I've been very lucky—I've been around a lot of other people who didn't have that, and that's a legacy I will carry forward.

Wright

How do you respond to the critics that life coaches and wellness coaches are usurping the turf of the mental health professionals?

Williams

I've had a lot of interviews on radio and newspaper about that. Now that the profession is over ten years old since it first started around 1996 when it really declared itself as a coaching profession, what I say is that most people in this country don't seek the services of a therapist because of the stigma of telling somebody you need therapy. It shouldn't be that way but it is!

Seventy percent of therapy clients are female, so that means that most men don't go to a therapist, yet we know that they could benefit from it. We also know that a lot of the people who might benefit from seeing a therapist don't really need therapy—they just need private confidential conversation about what it is that they want to change in their life. So why should that have a diagnostic label and require the services of a mental illness professional?

I think modern-day coaches are like philosophers and maybe the town priest or the older relative or the village elder who used to be available in tribal societies. Those kinds of people are not available anymore in modern culture. I think that mental health professionals need to know that when people seek and need proper professional treatment for depression, post-traumatic stress, bipolar disorders, and severe anxieties, etc., then they need to see a therapist. But when people just have problems in living and they are able to get coaching on how to get in motion and make some changes, then that's where coaching has come into play.

The good news is that therapists who want to train can do both! They can differentiate between when they offer coaching and when they offer therapy. The other coaches who don't have a therapy background need to learn how to stay in the coaching mode and not start coaching their clients in overcoming depression. We do a lot on training coaches to know when to refer their clients to mental health professionals.

I think life coaching really benefits both professions. Coaches will know when to refer to therapists, and therapists will need to know when to refer to coaches. The profession of coaching is not licensed, but it is self-regulated by those who join the International Coach Federation. We can talk a little bit more about that, but remember, professional consultants are not regulated either so the buyer needs to do his or her due diligence when hiring or engaging the services of a consultant or a professional coach.

Wright

It's interesting you would say that men and women as well need conversation. I had an important conversation some years ago with a man I admire, and he told me, "In this culture people don't communicate, they just take turns talking." I was wondering what you thought.

Williams

That's a great statement. I give training on the history and evolution of coaching as well as the future of coaching. The two biggest reasons that I think coaching has popped up as a new profession is the fact that there is a shortage of listening in our society, and it's worldwide. The world is so fast-paced and conversations are so short. We are used to the thirty-second soundbyte on television. We are used to drive-up windows and microwaves and Starbucks and text messaging with code—even the best friends you might have just aren't there long enough to really have conversation with you at a meaningful level when you need it. If you have a great spouse and great friends, you should give yourself a hug and give them a hug for that; but a coach is someone who can be there for you on a regular basis to listen—to really listen soulfully—to who you are and what you want.

The second reason that I think coaching popped up on the landscape is the lack of connection. It's similar to the shortage of listening. There was an article in the *Washington Post* reporting that Americans are more isolated today than they were ten years ago. People don't know their neighbors, they don't have close friends, and they don't feel connected. In the world of business more people are entrepreneurial and self-employed and transitory, so there's a lot of isolation. That's where having a personal coach has come in vogue because it fills that need; so connection and listening are big reasons.

Wright

Many critics say that this is an unregulated profession and that they believe it's deceptive to the public. How do you respond to those critics?

Williams

I love to educate them about that. As I said earlier, the field of consulting has never been regulated—anybody can claim to be a consultant. Some are charlatans and some are professional. Usually reputation precedes the consultant being hired, because you have to be able to deliver on what you promise.

Coaches are not snake oil salesmen, although I'll be the first to admit that like any hot profession it does attract its share of charlatans. The public needs to ask a potential coach, "Where have you trained? Do you have testimonials of clients who have worked with you?"

In this market today it's really important to ask the coach if he or she has trained at a school that's accredited by the International Coach Federation (ICF). That would get rid of the charge of deception because there are ethical guidelines that accredited coaches have to follow. Anybody can go out and call themselves a coach, and if they're a good listener maybe they could say, "I coached so-and-so"—but if you really want to hire a *professional* coach you need to make sure that the coach has trained with an organization that has quality standards and quality training. Most likely that means he or she is accredited by the ICF. To hire a coach means to hire someone who is either certified by the ICF or is on the path of being certified.

This is such a new profession; we've gone from having only 1,900 certified coaches worldwide in 2004, to over 3,000. We currently have over 14,000 members in the ICF—ten years ago we only had 200. It was a brand new membership organization in 1996. We currently have members in eighty countries, so it's truly a global profession. Even though it's unregulated it is ethically prescribed and membership does have its standards.

Wright

Let me ask you a question and see if I'm on the right track. After hearing you talk, I think it would have been helpful to me many, many years ago if I had had someone who was a coach who could have helped me. I didn't ever consider myself ill, so I never did feel the necessity to go to anyone to "fix" me. But what you're talking about is that you could have helped me determine those things I may not have thought about, avenues I may not have elected to travel, and options that I didn't have the right knowledge about to go through the correct doors. Is that what you are talking about?

Williams

In a sense, yes; that's pretty close. I think the idea of having a coach is that you may have a lot of great ideas, but having a conversation with a coach helps you make the right choices for you at that moment. Now, we all know you might make a choice and three months later you find out the choice wasn't the best one—but if you made it intelligently, if you made it weighed against all the other potential choices, then there really wasn't a "wrong" choice. All successful businesspeople out there—some of the successful millionaires and billionaires of the world—will tell you about mistakes they made. So mistakes are not bad, they are just choice points in your life.

A coach will not tell you what to do or what to choose or how to be, but a coach will ask powerful questions that will evoke from you your deepest thinking. Even if I were to say to you, "What do you want—what do you *really* want? How would you want your life to be different than it is today?" You would ponder that for a while and I would listen to your reaction for several minutes.

Coaching is not like having a conversation at Starbucks where your friend asks you what do you want and you say, "Hey, I want to get out of this job and I'd like to be retired." That's a good chat with a friend; a coach will go deeper. A coach will say, "What else? Tell me more." A coach will say, "So what have you thought about? What are your strengths? What gifts do you bring to this opportunity?" A coach will also say, "Why not?" You may want to move to Costa Rica and open a scuba diving shop, "Well, okay, why not? What stands in the way of that?" A coach won't say, "Sounds like a good idea, you should do that"—a coach will tell you, "If that's what you really want to do, let's talk about how to make that happen." Does that make sense?

Wright

Yes, and it sounds good too, by the way.

Williams

That's one of my dreams—being on an island—so I gave some of my own truth there.

Wright

You always seem to be involved in the creative and cutting edge of projects. Would you tell our readers what's next for Dr. Patrick Williams?

Williams

Oh boy, that is a good question. Every time I run into people, they actually ask me that question. They say things like, "Pat, I read about you in your newsletter; I see you in press releases. What the heck are you up to now?"

I'm excited to say that this is something new on my radar screen that I'm very excited about—I was just awarded the first Global Visionary Fellowship of the Foundation of Coaching. This is a new non-profit, neutral think-tank for coaching that is funded by a private family foundation. They chose me as their first Global Visionary Fellow because of a project I'm working on called Coaching the Global Village.

We plan to take the coach approach in group format and in training leaders to third world or developing nations, and really go into rural villages in India, Africa, Costa Rica, Peru, you name it. So far I have an advisory board of eight members. I'm putting together the meat of a proposal to go after bigger money to actually pilot this in 2007. It's very, very exciting and it has attracted the interest of some high profile people; I'm really excited about it. I can see that project becoming something in the next decade that takes more of my time than running my training school and I would welcome that.

I'm an old hippy from the 1960s. We had desires to change the world. There's a quote I like by E. B. White that says, "I arise each morning torn between a desire to improve or *save* the world, and a desire to enjoy or *savor* the world. This makes it hard to plan my day!" That's my motive—I want to enjoy life and have balanced time, but I also really want to save the world! Not individually, but collectively. This is done by empowering people to live more purposefully, individually, in their relationships, community, and in the global context as well.

Wright

What a great conversation. I really appreciate the time that you've taken with me today to answer all these questions. You've given me a lot of things to think about and I'm sure our readers are going to be impacted just the same!

Williams

Well I appreciate it; I love talking about this, it's my passion and my life.

Wright

Today we've been talking with Dr. Patrick Williams, often referred to as "Dr. Pat." He's one of the early pioneers of coaching, and as we've found out in this conversation, he deserves the title of Ambassador of Life Coaching.

Dr. Williams, thank you so much for being with us today on *Speaking of Success.*

Williams

You're very welcome!

About the Author

One of the early pioneers of coaching, Dr. Patrick Williams MCC began executive coaching as part of his psychology practice in 1990. In 1998 he founded the Institute for Life Coach Training, an ICF Accredited Coach Training Program. He speaks worldwide on topics of living purposefully, coaching for global change, wellness coaching, and the coach approach in leadership. He has written dozens of articles and been interviewed on television and radio. Pat was awarded the first Global Visionary Fellowship by the Foundation of Coaching for his coaching the Global Village project, a non-profit organization to take the coach approach to developing villages on the planet. You may view his media kit and learn about training at http://www.lifecoachtraining.com

He is co-author of *Therapist as Life Coach: Transforming Your Practice* (2002); *Total Life Coaching: 50+ Life Lessons, Skills, and Techniques to Enhance your Practice and Your Life* (2005); *Law and Ethics of Coaching: How to Solve and Avoid Difficult Problems in Your Practice (2006);* and *Becoming a Professional Life Coach: Lessons from The Institute for Life Coach Training (2007).*

Dr. Patrick Williams
Master Certified Coach, Chief Energizing Officer
Institute for Life Coach Training
17 Lakeside Drive
Palm Coast, FL 32137
Phone: 386.597.4592
E-mail: Pat@LifeCoachTraining.com
www.LifeCoachTraining.com

Chapter 14

ANDREW MORRIS

THE INTERVIEW

David Wright (Wright)

Today we're talking with Andrew Morris. Andrew brings over sixteen years of experience in investments and retirement planning. As a top marketing executive for one of the largest financial institutions in the world he has honed his skills through his dealings with investment bankers, financial advisors, accountants, and attorneys. Andrew brings a wealth of knowledge and financial strategies to the podium. He has spoken to such groups as the National Association of MBAs, the Society of Chartered Financial Planning, the Association of Insurance and Financial Advisors, the Women's Society of Realtors, and several chapters of the New Jersey and Pennsylvania Society of CPAs. He's a member of the National Association of Black MBAs and Professional Speakers Bureau.

Andrew Morris welcome to *Speaking of Success.*

Andrew Morris (Morris)

Good afternoon, how are you?

Wright

Just fine, thank you. Andrew, every time I ask someone to define success I get as many definitions of success as people I ask, so how do you define success?

Morris

Well, I would say that success is a state of mind and involves various combinations of thought that culminate in the idea that someone is considered successful.

Success can be measured by oneself and also by how one is perceived by others in society. I would define success in several different ways:

a. Achievements—positions one may have achieved in life and in one's career.
b. Spiritual and physical—a strong belief in a higher power and maintaining physical strength.
c. Family—completeness and health of the family unit.
d. Financial—how much money one makes and how that wealth is manifested in terms of material possessions.
e. Power—the ability to lead and empower others as well as to influence others to follow you.

Although on some levels, true success encompasses some measure of each of the five definitions noted above, I would like to explore three of these definitions of success in more detail here.

To me, family success means achieving a harmonious state within your family life. This means ensuring that there is balance between the time you spend with your children, spouse, or significant other, and work. You need to make sure that your children feel loved and happy; that you have created a good foundation for them in which you have instilled some core values that will contribute to their success within their future careers and family.

Financial success is achieved once you have reached the pinnacle of your profession. The money you make enables you to obtain material possessions such as cars, homes, and other things. This financial success enables you to move in circles you would have otherwise not have access to if you weren't earning a high income. Financial success may be a goal for some as this enables one to provide for oneself and one's family. Spiritual and physical success is the last definition of success I would like to discuss here, although there are two other forms of success in my definition above. In order to achieve success in any form I strongly believe in the importance of embracing both spirituality and physical strength and harmony.

I attribute a big part of my success to my strong belief in God. This has given me the confidence to believe that I can achieve anything I set out to achieve. In the face of adversity, I have found that prayer and a strong belief in a higher power have propelled me in the right direction. Also, my mental strength in achieving my goals, as it relates to success, comes from my physical strength that I enrich by working out and maintaining my endurance skills as a former professional athlete.

In conclusion, there are various aspects of success and in my opinion each is interrelated in one way or another. We each need to examine our desires and characteristics to determine which measures of success are most important to us. For me again, the three main aspects of success are: family, financial, spiritual, and physical. Each of these has had a significant impact on helping me achieve and measure my success, as well as shaping how well I have dealt with and overcome adversity.

Wright

What would you say is the biggest contribution to your professional success?

Morris

I truly believe that I would not be as successful as I am today without the people and experiences I have had in my life that have molded and influenced me to be who I am today.

Most important in this network of people are my parents who have taught me to go after everything I have wanted. They instilled in me strong values and the confidence to reach and exceed my potential.

Throughout my career and my life experiences I have encountered people on either side of the spectrum—those who have encouraged and mentored me as well as those who have not always been so positive. Each of these encounters and experiences has strengthened my resolve and desire to achieve my goals and objectives.

Of course I should also pay homage to my strong work ethic, which I think has also been a strong contributor to my personal success. I believe that one must work hard to reap the benefits of success; without hard work there is no pay off. If it means putting in those extra hours when you are tired, you must be willing to do that. If you have to go the extra mile on a project, then that should be second nature. Those in positions who could potentially impact whether you are successful or able to achieve your goals will always be present to make a judgment on whether you win or lose (this could be your boss, clients, customers, vendors, etc.). Again, I believe this strong work ethic was instilled in me at a very early age by my parents, both of whom worked very hard all of their lives. Their hard work paid off in contributing to their becoming successful; they became "self-made" by doing things honestly and by helping others along the way.

Although in my situation a strong work ethic is a product of my background and upbringing, I do believe that this is also something you could learn or teach yourself if you have a strong desire and incentive to achieve a given measure of success in your chosen specialty/profession.

Wright

Aside from personal role models, who are the people who have served as your role models for success?

Morris

Well, my personal role models include my parents since I believe you should look for good role models at home first if they are available to you. Today too many young people are very quick to name professional athletes and musicians as their role models. However, there are other well known individuals who have been a big influence in my life, career, and ultimately in my success.

These role models include the great civil rights leader, Dr. Martin Luther King. He paved the way and changed the destiny of African-Americans and other minorities by knocking down the barriers that held minorities back from achieving their full potential. He opened doors to help American citizens—black, brown, and white—look at each other as being equal without a separation based on skin color. He did this in a non-violent, definitive, and persuasive way. Dr. King got across a point that society as a whole still continues to try to understand and develop and expand upon today. In part, this is what has driven me and fueled my passion for public speaking—Dr. King was a great orator. As you know, he was an ordained pastor and I have listened to many of his speeches, specifically his *"I have a dream speech"* over the years, which remains very powerful and moving to me. These speeches have touched me as well as others from around the world and they have and will continue to influence my life tremendously.

In addition to Martin Luther King, Napoleon Hill has influenced my life greatly. Mr. Hill's book, *Think and Grow Rich,* helped give me the direction and mindset I needed to stay on the road to success by stating what things to do and what things not to do. This remarkable book helped me decide once and for all how I was to accomplish my goals. Mental strength and aptitude is crucial if you are going to be successful in life. In other words, by controlling your mind you can control your destiny.

I absorbed and applied Napoleon Hill's famous thirteen principles for unbridled success. Three of his main principles are the foundation for my success: faith, knowledge, and persistence.

1. Faith is the state of mind that may be induced or created by affirmation. By continually summoning a mental image of yourself already having accomplished your main desire, you will muster the faith you need. Faith is vital to accomplishment.
2. Knowledge is power only to the extent that it's organized into a definite plan of action and directed to a definite end.
3. Persistence is simply the power of will. When properly combined, willpower and desire make an irresistible pair. For me, persistence has stood as the difference between success and failure.

Wright

So what do you think are the biggest obstacles people face in trying to become successful?

Morris

The path to success can be a challenging one. The negative influences come in many forms, which can include external sources like individuals who don't want you to achieve the success you desire whether consciously or unconsciously. But I believe the biggest obstacle is sabotaging oneself. There are so many different mediums around such as television, radio, and the Internet, which serve to often clutter our minds by providing distractions that then take us off track and leave us unfocused on our goals.

Additionally, I believe that lack of organization and/or lack of discipline are some of the biggest drawbacks facing many people who may otherwise have the qualities to become very successful. These individuals may never achieve their fullest potential because they get distracted; hence they do not achieve their ultimate goals in life. As I mentioned earlier, there are a number of different levels of success, but in order to achieve these levels of success one must set goals and objectives, have a clear and concise plan that is easy to follow, and stay focused and on track by being determined, consistent, and disciplined.

Wright

So how did you become successful in your chosen field?

Morris

It all goes back to my personal role models—my mom and dad. They always gave me the motivation and the enthusiasm I needed to feel confident in my abilities. They gave me the necessary encouragement telling me that I could do anything I put my mind to. Not only did they instill in me a strong work ethic as I had mentioned, they were always available to provide me with the encouragement and necessary pick-me-ups when I needed it and when things were not going as smoothly as I would have wanted.

I also don't want to underestimate the power of perseverance. Knowing that my chosen profession in financial services is extremely competitive, through discipline and a lot of very hard work I have cultivated and excelled in my motivational speaking, which I have purposefully incorporated into my workload. Thus, in order for me stay successful and several steps ahead of the competition, I have to constantly update my product knowledge base (remaining cutting edge) and my oratory and persuasive skills; naturally, this takes hard work.

I can relate my competitive nature and desire to be very hardworking to my days as a competitive athlete in college. Growing up I had a sports career throughout high school and college and eventually I became a minor league baseball player. I attribute this to being disciplined and to a great deal of hard work. I would often ask myself the same question that I now put to the audience: "If you're going to persevere and if there's a setback, do you just give up or do you come back from that setback and continue to focus on your goals?"

Wright

You talked a few minutes ago about the importance of balance in all areas of your life to ensure success. How do you balance your success with your life?

Morris

Well, it certainly is a delicate balance, however, family success is extremely important to me as well as the other forms of success I have talked about. I try to balance time at work with the time I spend with my family.

The quality of your own existence as well as the need for your children to spend quality time with you creates the need for balance. In order for them to become productive, healthy, and happy human beings in society it is necessary to show them that life is not just about work. It's about having passion for what you do in order to make a successful living; but there's a time for play and there's a time for work.

I achieve balance in my life by spending time with my family and friends either by going on vacation, taking a trip, or maybe by just reading a book while sitting near the fireplace, or perhaps just having conversation. I enjoy and find outdoor activities invigorating; thus my family and I will go horseback riding or hiking. Most recently we went whitewater rafting. All these things, whether with family or friends, have helped me to remain balanced and to stay very competitive while at work.

Wright

You talked about people who have influenced your life such as your mother and father, Martin Luther King, and Napoleon Hill; so how can people help other people succeed?

Morris

A key component of humanity is the ability to serve. Service can come in many different forms, so it is important to realize that true success also comes with one's ability to bring others up the ladders of success. It is important to understand that true success comes from how you extend your hand to help someone else and give back to the community. This is known as "paying it forward"—helping others to benefit from your knowledge, experience, and success so they can also achieve a measure of success for themselves.

I believe that the act of giving is a major characteristic of a person who has faith in God. The blessings you're able to give to other people come back to you two-fold if not ten-fold many times.

Wright

Would you tell our readers a little bit about what drives you to be successful?

Morris

My personal drive toward success comes from my underlying desire to make sure that my children and family are provided for. A successful life is often determined by the quality of life one has and whether one can feel good about oneself. There are many factors that drive individuals toward achieving success, including money, material possessions, and recognition from society at large. My motivation is family.

No matter what your individual circumstances are, you can succeed and accomplish any goal that you set your mind to. It boils down to having passion for what you do and the determination to do just that. Whether you are in financial services, sports, entertainment, medicine, communications, or public service, if you are driven and feel good about yourself because you have accomplished your goals, then this is success. When I come home every day I think about making a better life for my family and friends and that's what keeps me going.

Wright

So what obstacles have you had to overcome in your chosen profession to remain successful?

Morris

The financial services field is very competitive. One must continually attempt to differentiate oneself from various competitors who are marketing their products and services. As an African-American man building a career in this field I have experienced many obstacles that I have had to overcome with poise. Some of these include innuendos made by peers, employers, or clients that I wasn't capable of excelling, perhaps because of my race. Naturally, this just provided me with a greater incentive to excel, by adding fuel to my fire and further developing my desire for success.

Whenever someone says you can't do something or doubts your ability, then you have the opportunity to work harder and prove them wrong. You make sure that your skills exceed their level of expectation. Regardless of the circumstances, whenever there is an opportunity or an opening that may lead to success you should always take advantage of that opportunity. "Success is the result of preparation and taking advantage of opportunities that may come your way."

Another obstacle I have had to overcome was my initial fear of public speaking. Although I have become more comfortable with my ability to speak to audiences of any size, early in my career I would feel sick to my stomach before a presentation. That anxiety has since subsided due to continued practice, practice, and more practice through the years.

As a public speaker, I have honed my oratory and communication skills in order to enable me to effectively articulate and interact with an audience at the highest level so that I can inspire and influence them to go in a particular direction. Regardless of the circumstances or the audience, I know—based on my background and knowledge—that I can deliver. Regardless of the color of my skin, nothing will hold me back or keep me from succeeding.

As long as you are self-assured and are confident in your abilities you will overcome any adversity you may face.

Wright

You have spoken about passion being the driving force in your life and that it's one of the main factors in attaining success. Is passion alone truly enough?

Morris

Passion alone is a significant barometer for you to use in determining whether you will achieve the level of success you crave or desire. However, passion alone cannot be the only driving force, although it will help in determining your level of commitment and drive in achieving your goals. Without passion you're not going to want to get up in the morning or go to work or hone your skills or provide for your family. If you have passion, it's going to help you grow to become a better person so that you're able to better communicate with your family and others. As you grow as a person mentally, physically, and spiritually this passion spills over into all the different areas of your life. Passion is definitely a key component; it's not the only component, but it's definitely a key component that will help you get on your road to success.

Wright

So how did you begin speaking and why have you chosen overcoming adversity as your main topic?

Morris

One of the main requirements of my profession as a marketing executive within the financial services industry is to give presentations about the financial products and services that my company offers to clients, therefore communication skills are extremely important. As a result of this, I found that I not only enjoy speaking in public but I am also very good at it.

Speaking on overcoming adversity is a subject that is very near and dear to me because of the experiences I have endured in my life and career. I believe that this is a very important subject that will help others who are navigating through their careers and personal challenges. Hopefully I can help others realize that there is always a light at the end of the tunnel, and success in all its forms is definitely achievable.

Wright

As a parent, is it important to you to be a role model to your children as well a role model to others?

Morris

Absolutely. I have two beautiful children, Brooke and Gregory. Gregory is a National Honor student and my daughter is an A student in middle school. As a parent, I have laid a foundation to help them succeed. I believe that I have also given them the necessary tools to be successful in life. There are going to be some setbacks and obstacles in life, but if they remain focused and determined, they will achieve their goals.

My belief is that a strong foundation for success should also include a solid education through the post-graduate level. This will definitely make the path to success less challenging and more achievable.

What I try to do through various mentorship programs is to help others along the way. Living what I believe to be a giving and charitable life includes interaction with my own family and kids as well as with other kids and friends of my children. I have always heard "you're doing a great job" or "your children seem so well grounded" or "you guys seem like you're having so much fun." So I do think that being a role model doesn't just apply to your own children—it's always important to reach out to other children who may not have good role models in their lives and in some way try to make their paths to success easier.

Wright

Would you tell our readers what a Marketing Director at a top tier financial services firm like yours does?

Morris

As a Marketing Director at a top tier financial services firm I am responsible for bringing in millions of dollars in annual sales revenues. I do this by making presentations to our institutional investment clients regarding the financial products and services that my company offers.

During these presentations I educate potential clients about the reasons why they should recommend my company's products and services to their individual and institutional clients. The format of these presentations is either formal or through written and/or slide presentations, and sometimes an audio presentation is provided. My goal during these presentations is to market and sell services to assist individuals in understanding the benefits of retirement planning, tax deferred investing, and estate planning. These are the specific aspects of the financial services industry that are the key components of my work.

For those considering a career in the financial services industry, namely in marketing products related to retirement and estate planning and tax deferred investing, it is important to realize that most likely you will need to have a background and some direct knowledge about the various types of investment products. Obtaining a master's degree in marketing, and gaining experience in the field is an excellent starting point. This should contribute to your potential success in financial services. These things have helped me succeed in my field. Additionally, another important aspect of succeeding in this field is to obtain the relevant certifications and licenses such as the Certified Financial Planner (CFP), the Series 7 license (registered securities representative) and the Certified Investment Management Analyst (CIMA). You should also know that a Marketing Director's job is very entrepreneurial and therefore it is like owning your own business. You are in charge of your own destiny and the outcome of your success. Inevitably, in this position I am presenting and selling my company's products and services to clients.

Wright

Would you say that when people follow their passion and excel, then does the passion bring success or does the success bring more passion?

Morris

I believe it works both ways. The more passion you have for a field or specialty in which you have an interest, the greater the likelihood that you will succeed in this area/profession. Now, as I had mentioned earlier, passion alone will not lead to success. Other factors must be present to solidify this success; you can excel in an area in which you have a great deal of passion but you shouldn't expect to succeed every time. Also, it is possible to have several passions and only to succeed in one or none. However, if hard work and a strong work ethic accompany this passion then the likelihood for success increases. It is also possible to have a lot of passion in an area/profession, achieve success, and then lose the passion and drive to continue once success has been achieved and your ultimate goals have been reached. In this case one might seek other passions and explore the idea of achieving success in another area. Therefore, in this instance, success may bring more passion and vice versa.

Having that passion initially, and continuing to encourage it to grow throughout your career, is a catalyst for the beginning of what success could bring. You should expect that you will have some failures along the way and if you take the time to learn from these failures they will help you become more successful in whatever you choose to do. Thus when failure happens—and it will—you will not be discouraged and you will still have that passion and drive to succeed. Most successful individuals have had many failures and attribute their greatest triumphs to these setbacks.

Passion will continue to keep you focused. As you achieve your ultimate goals I believe success creates the possibility of more passion, which may lead to you to becoming even more successful.

Wright

So what do you think makes your perspective unique?

Morris

That is an interesting question. I believe that as an African-American man who has excelled within an industry that is not particularly open to African-Americans, that I bring a unique perspective and insight into achieving success in the face of adversity. This is certainly a contributing factor to the reasons I speak on overcoming adversity as a part of my motivational speeches.

My perspective is unique because, due to my Caribbean background, I have had a chance to better appreciate life. Growing up, as a child I would often take trips with my parents back and forth to Jamaica. I understood at an early age what poverty and despair was, since the high unemployment and economic state of the country was so poor. It led people to crime and homelessness, which I saw first-hand.

I believe that experiencing adversity in life, regardless of your profession or career path, brings you into harmony with those who share a different perspective on achieving success. Most successful people, you will find, have failed many times prior to their achieving great success. Overcoming adversity and being able to adapt to various situations has helped them stay focused and not give up on their goals and objectives.

Perseverance is a very important characteristic of success. Individuals need to know that in spite of setbacks they may experience on their road to success, the skills and the ability necessary to overcome adversity is inherent in their beings. These experiences will only make them stronger.

As an African-American, being able to succeed in a predominantly Caucasian male industry has definitely helped me to know how to overcome adversity, even when people may have thought I would never be able to do the things I've done in life. Perseverance, a strong work ethic, supportive parents, friends, and family have all contributed and continue to contribute to my financial, career, emotional, family, and spiritual success.

Wright

Well Andrew, I really do appreciate all the time you've spent with me this afternoon answering all these questions. I certainly have learned a lot. Your life seems extremely interesting and I congratulate you on your success.

Morris

Thank you very much.

Wright

Today we've been talking with Andrew Morris. He is a Regional Vice President and retirement specialist for a AAA rated insurance company headquartered in Boston, Massachusetts. Andrew is a licensed continuing education instructor in the states of Pennsylvania, New Jersey, and Delaware. He graduated from Iona College in New Rochelle, New York, with a bachelor's degree in Finance and obtained his MBA from Sacred Heart University in Fairfield, Connecticut, with an emphasis in Marketing. He brings a unique combination of success both as a former professional athlete and sales representative within the investment industry. He travels the region providing both seminars and training for all his clients.

Andrew, thank you so much for being with us today on *Speaking of Success.*

Morris

Thank you very much. You have a great day.

About the Author

ANDREW MORRIS is an accomplished professional speaker, keynote presenter, motivator, and author. Andrew holds degrees in Business, including an MBA in Marketing, and he holds several professional certifications. Andrew is a frequent guest speaker at professional and industry association meetings. He is an esteemed member of the International Who's Who Association of Business Professionals, and has made several television and radio appearances, speaking on the topics of charitable gift-giving, mentoring, workplace diversity, overcoming adversity, estate planning, and retirement planning. Andrew brings his life experiences and philosophies from the corporate world, entrepreneurship, and private business to help at risk children through mentoring and providing motivational presentations. Andrew enjoys painting, golf, and any outdoor fitness activities in his spare time. He is also a certified scuba diver and enjoys a good glass of wine while reading.

Andrew Morris
795 Route 70 E., Suite E #176
Marlton, NJ 08053
Phone: 609.614.7712
E-mail: Andrew.Morris2006@comcast.net